Swollen Appetite

A memoir by
Sandra Austin Mello

This is a work of memoir, based on the author's memory. The events depicted are accurate to the best of her knowledge, though some may remember them differently. Some names and identifying details have been changed to protect the privacy of the individuals described.

Copyright ©2021 Sandra Austin Mello
Library of Congress

Joan of Arc
Words and Music by Leonard Cohen
Copyright ©1971 Sony Songs LLC
All Rights Administered by Sony Music Publishing, 424 Church Street, Suite 1200, Nashville, TN 37219 International Copyright Secured All Rights Reserved
Reprinted by Permission of Hal Leonard LLC
PR1578990 - permission to use the lyrics "Swollen Appetite"

All rights reserved. No part of this book may be reproduced or transmitted in any form or by any means, electronic or mechanical, including photocopying, recording, or by any information storage or retrieval system now known or hereafter invented–except by a reviewer who may quote brief passages in a review to be printed in a magazine or newspaper–without permission in writing from the author.

ISBN 978-0-9997330-2-8

Cover illustration ©Brian Mello
For additional materials and contact information:
sandraaustinmello.com

There are many provocative subjects within these pages including alcohol use disorder, drugs, sex, HIV/AIDS, suicidal ideation, reckless and destructive behavior, and lots and lots of cussing.

For all the hands that held mine.

Swollen Appetite

Contents

Prologue

1. Swollen Appetite 1
2. I Love You. Who Is This? 19
3. His Voice Rising from My Throat 33
4. Two-Drink Minimum 39
5. Journal Entry, October 5, 1992 49
6. You're Just Getting Started 51
7. 28 White Doves 56
8. Night-Blooming Cereus 64
9. Laid a Golden Egg 79
10. Three Decades of Me 91
11. Why Nashville? 97

12. Dear Nashville, You're Someone Else's Dream   103
13. Ashes in My Mouth   123
14. Gave Directions to Keanu Reeves   134
15. Arrangements   147
16. Box Full of Wires   154
17. Not My Last Drink   165
18. When the Universe Gives You Cake, Eat it   172
19. Pick Up Your Bed and Walk   183
20. God-Given Talent   188
21. My Toes Curled in My Boots   195
22. You Can't Buy Experience   207
23. First Date   212
24. Oakland   218

Acknowledgement

Prologue

A twenty-nine-year-old woman is God's greatest achievement. A drunk twenty-nine-year-old woman is more powerful than God.

Just ask one.

There was a singer I met in 1992 when I first moved to San Francisco. She had a glass jaw and a wild story. An arrow had pierced her heart and pinned her to the wall.

To stop the bleeding, she poured bottles of whiskey over the wound. It worked. The hole was cauterized. With two hands she wrenched the arrow from her body and her song became a bellow. Hell-bent, she chased down the archer.

I worried about her. Wrung my hands in plain sight.

Until the day her glass jaw returned to sand. Hollowed out by fury, she blew across the shore and her song became notes in a bottle washed out to sea.

It was a long time ago, but I can't forget her. I want to tell her how sorry I am that I wasn't a better friend. And thank her for sharing her glory. She was a honeycomb sunrise that spilled over my days and hardened into memories. A candle stuck in a drawer.

This is how she found her wick.

Chapter 1 - Swollen Appetite

I was living in a little yellow house on Chalcedony Street in San Diego, California, with my husband, Brad, and our cat, Nellie. Nellie liked to hang out with me in the front yard while I sunbathed in my French-cut neon-green bikini and studied Russian political history for classes at San Diego State. When Nellie got too hot, she'd crawl under the blanket I'd spread out on the lawn—an inching lump beside my textbooks, notes, and beer. One day while I studied and she hunted in the flowers, a bee stung her on the nose. She zigzagged backward across the yard, maybe to get out from under the sting and undo the pain. She slunk down and hid in the bushes and would not let me help her.

Then the Improv comedy club transferred Brad to Irvine, and we moved away from the ocean.

A year and a few months later, I drove our charcoal-gray Toyota pickup truck to an Irvine bank and inserted our pearly-white Optima card into the ATM. I surprised myself by typing in a much bigger number than I'd intended, not sure if I could milk an ATM with a credit card. Lo and behold, hundred-dollar bills—twenty of them, to be exact—shuffled out of the slot into my trembling, twenty-nine-year-old hand. The year was 1992. I was being sneaky, stockpiling, getting my ducks in a row so I could do what I wanted without guff or repudiation. Twisted up and frustrated, I wanted to get out from under the strains of my marriage.

Tall, tan, and fashionable, Brad had been offered a promotion in Los Angeles. I could not see a life for myself in LA because LA belonged to actors and models. How could I—a short, studious woman—compete? And I hated the traffic and the smog. Brad's future in entertainment management brightened under the LA glitz, but my ambitions couldn't grow in his shadow, and I had wasted my twenties on him.

In my marrow, I knew I could write songs and had a strong voice, but I feared I'd waited too long to act on my desire to be a singer. Nonetheless, I struggled very little with Brad's decision to accept the job offer in LA. He needed that job, and I needed to move back to San Francisco, where we had lived for a few fraught months at the beginning of our marriage. San Francisco had prodded me in a way I liked. It provoked what I had secretly wanted to be all of my life: an artist. Maybe even a rock star. My precarious ambition had so far stayed hidden, and untested.

Brad didn't need to know a goddamn thing about my fantasy life. It's not that I didn't love him; I just didn't trust our relationship enough to change in front of him. I might make ugly noises and drink too much in the discovery process. And then he might make fun of me, ask me to stop singing—or, worse, ask me to drink less. The nights I didn't work at the Irvine Improv, but he did, I drank a full black bottle of sparkling Freixenet from Trader Joe's and wriggled around on the living room floor in front of the stereo, singing along to Holly and the Italians or Sinéad O'Connor. The more I drank, the more certain I became about my singing ability. Before Brad got home from work, I made sure to bury the empty wine bottle deep in the curbside trash can. Then I'd drink a beer or two from the six-pack in the fridge so there'd be plenty for him and he would think I'd only had a few.

The idea that I could leave my husband fueled a fire that burned our marriage to cinders. I announced that I would not be moving to LA with him. He was surprised—or maybe relieved, I'm not sure—but neither of us tried very hard to stay together and make things work. He jumped to worrying more about what to tell our friends and his parents. Or so it seemed. Determined to leave right away, I tried not to be a jerk and reveal my eagerness to get on with things. Plus, I wanted to be gone before he saw the credit card statement.

A few days after taking the money from the ATM, I caught a ride with friends to the suburb of Walnut Creek, then boarded the squeaky, swaying BART train and rode into San Francisco to search for an apartment. In my mind, the City by the Bay was the Land of Oz for artists. The truck and the credit card bill I left with Brad.

Swollen Appetite

San Francisco is the most beautiful city in the United States. San Francisco, where the roots of ancient redwood trees try in vain to hold the fault lines still. Nature favors this craggy crook of the Pacific and sculpted one of her most iconic shores. Before the native Ohlone and Ramaytush people, before the Spanish missionaries and conquistadors, before the gold miners' shacks and bordellos, and before the bridges, train tracks, grand hotels, big banks, and Victorian houses, San Francisco was dressed and ready in a plunging coastline wrapped in a velvet-fog shrug.

  She is haloed unlike any place I have ever seen. The rays of light slant through the mist and band like the rings of Saturn. The light makes spiderwebs sing. The way the Northern California light twines through the branches of cypress, redwood, and eucalyptus changed the way I see the color gold. The light is more golden than a trophy and more seductive than wealth. No longer did the word "gold" evoke the soft metal of my wedding ring. A few months in, I pawned that useless band for eight bucks and bought a twelve-pack of Schaefer beer with the wrinkled bills.

  That light showed itself after the sun burned away the fog. Oh, how I needed the fog! It softened sharp edges, shielded me, and let me sleep during the day while I worked at night. The shroud tempered The City's charms, which tried to tease my heart out of my rib cage and knock my fool head off. Folks had been flocking to San Francisco to reinvent themselves since the Gold Rush. Legend had it that if you lived in San Francisco for too long, you'd lose your mind. I lived there from 1992 until 1997, and the legend came true. I found the right place at the right time to fall apart.

Heading to San Francisco on my own, without Brad, took its place in a long line of rash decisions on my part, often involving men and moving. Case in point: on our first date, I accepted Brad's marriage proposal on the sidewalk outside a Thai restaurant in Los Angeles where I ate pad see ew, a chewy wide-noodle dish, for the first time. We were attending a joint birthday party for the comedian Hugh "You Mock What You Fear" Fink and MTV VJ Martha Quinn. Over a smoke on the sidewalk alongside Fairfax Avenue, he popped the question. I said yes. Brad changed five bucks into quarters and pumped them into a phone booth outside the restaurant to tell his brother the news before we went back inside and told everyone within earshot. The proximity to famous people excited me and made me feel special, as if their celebrity shine illuminated me as well. Life with this man looked brighter than the drunk and dramatic last five years I'd spent living with a different wrong person.

    I enjoyed our first date enough not to question things too rigorously. One hot afternoon, somewhere in the middle of our three-week engagement, I lay on a plastic chaise and worked on my tan. My fiancé surfaced through a spray of apartment complex pool water, glistening and tawny, his wet hair down to his shoulders like a sweaty rocker. Even though I doubted our marriage was made for eternity, it seemed to have potential. That night, while T Bone Burnett played on the CD player and sang about the killer moon, I tried to get into Brad's pants. He sighed and said not to worry, that he was hung like a horse but thought it would be super sexy and kind of kinky to wait to have sex until we were married. We wed on August 8, 1988, in Las Vegas, twenty-one days after our first date, with thirty or so of our friends and coworkers—including Brad's brother and his fiancée—in attendance. After we kissed, the movie theme song from *Rocky* rang out over the Chapel of the Bells' loudspeakers and I thanked all the "active participants in our life" for being a part of this momentous occasion. We hurried to our Vegas room to change out of our cool but ridiculously warm wedding clothes: I had worn a long-sleeved form-fitting black dress, and Brad a black dress shirt and pleated, cuffed trousers. We consummated our vows like it was a chore—I wasn't thrilled, but since we both wanted to drink champagne and party with our pals already celebrating by the pool, I bucked up. A pattern began: hanging out with our friends would always be more exciting than being intimate.

Comedy clubs were hitting their heyday in the late 1980s. A few weeks post-wedding, the Improv sent us to San Francisco to get a new club up and running. The location was a few blocks east of the Powell Street cable car line and the upscale department stores on Union Square—Saks, Neiman Marcus, Tiffany's, Bloomingdale's, Gump's—yet in those few blocks the neighborhood turned grittier. We remodeled a basement beneath the Jack in the Box on the grimy corner of Mason and Geary, across from the American Conservatory Theater. On the landing of the steps leading down to the future nightclub, a homeless man watched while we turned the moldy basement into a showroom, stocked the bar, and set up the office. We called him the quarter man because all he asked for was quarters. Shirtless, with a dirty blanket wrapped around his lower half, he asked, "Quarter? Got a quarter?" all the live-long day, until the club opened and he shuffled to a different set of steps across the street.

We spent our three-month stint in San Francisco in a studio apartment on the second floor of a 1930s building at the corner of Post and Taylor. I looked out from a window I'd taped a Johnny Thunders poster over instead of investing in curtains. Sex workers milled around the nearby newsstand. When it wasn't too cold, I sat on the fire escape (my first!) and smoked. Opposite the newsstand, the Pacific Union building hovered grandly on the incline, three stories of brown brick and ivy that housed a private Republican men's club. This neighborhood, known as the Tendernob, shook one hand with the Tenderloin, a neighborhood filled with vice and poverty, while the other hand accepted tips at the entrances of Nob Hill luxury hotels.

In those ninety days, the city ensnared me. Distracted by its beauty, a ropy pile of longing coiled inside me. On a daylong walk with Bob Nickman, a stand-up comedian who would go on to write for successful television shows like *The Drew Carey Show* and *Freaks and Geeks*, I complained about my unsatisfying creative life. At the top of a steep hill, we admired the way the old Italian neighborhood of North Beach terraced down to the sapphire bay dotted with white sailboats and ferries shuttling back and forth to Alcatraz Island. Bob paused, then said something along the lines of, "It must be hard for someone born with blonde hair and blue eyes to languish so."

Fast-forward to early 1992. I arrived in San Francisco after saying goodbye to my life and marriage in Southern California. I got off the BART at Powell Street and rode the escalator up from Hallidie Plaza, dodging pigeons and panhandlers on my way to meet my friend Chloe who worked at a nearby boutique hotel. "GOD SEES ALL" was stenciled on a sandwich board that hung heavy from the shoulders of a man with a megaphone. I wondered when the threat of going to hell had lost its ferociousness. A line of tourists waited at the cable car turnaround in shorts and hastily purchased sweatshirts. Nine decades of mercantile signage clashed, uneven and slapdash, and clamored for my attention.

After Chloe's shift ended, we went back to the Victorian flat on Fulton Street she shared with her boyfriend, the comic Tom Rhodes. A gobsmacking view of Alamo Square filled their living-room picture window. Chloe smelled like cigarettes and perfume. A curly bob crested her bronzed jawline, and she spoke in a glorious French accent. She had been the kickboxing champion of Paris a few years prior. Tom had long, curly brown hair and moved more like a lead singer in a 1970s rock band than a comedian—didn't matter whether he was on stage or walking to the corner store. This absurdly attractive couple let me crash on their hardwood floor while I searched for an apartment. They showed me the sights of San Francisco, Sausalito, and the Marin Headlands from the red leather interior of Tom's mint-condition vintage Cadillac. To keep it clean and off the street, Tom rented a garage from a friend who lived two blocks over. Being escorted in such style by such cool people through Golden Gate Park, past the Panhandle and the 1990s version of hippies, down California Street, past Anton LaVey's infamous black house, and over the Golden Gate Bridge with its Art Deco towers held together by a million rivets gave me an insider's view of the city. In the evenings at sunset, we watched the looming fog swirl through the tops of massive redwoods and eucalyptus trees—a Hitchcockian landscape—and drank wine and smoked cigarettes as we discussed the local comedy and alternative music scenes.

A few blocks away from my friends' flat, at the corner of Golden Gate Avenue and Steiner Street, I found the studio apartment of my dreams. Better than my dreams, because I had never seen this kind of apartment before. It was huge and old, with French doors that separated the dining room from the living area, high ceilings with ornate moldings and a crown-shaped chandelier, a bay window, and a silver-painted metal radiator. Covered in the original black and pink tile and with an intact ceramic claw-foot tub, the bathroom screamed Art Deco. The galley kitchen had been remodeled on the cheap in the '70s and the avocado-green, patterned linoleum was worn and busy. But who cared? I didn't intend to spend too much time cooking. The low-pile, dark-brown carpet in the living room hid cigarette ash and spilled wine. Since I did not have a car, but I did have a cat, I appreciated the veterinarian's office right across the street. The unit was one of eight apartments on the third floor of a ten-story building erected after the great earthquake and fire of 1906. The white outline of a body was painted on the sidewalk below, forever commemorating where some poor soul had jumped to their death. That detail seemed especially cool and urban. But the cost intimidated me: $525 a month.

I bought the rental agent a box of fancy donuts and pestered the living daylights out of her, hoping to qualify. It worked. I headed back to SoCal and, with the help of a few friends in Irvine, including my soon-to-be-ex, Brad, I filled a small U-Haul with my things. We moved Nellie the cat and myself into our beautiful new studio.

That first night there, the moving crew and I ate mushrooms and roamed the Haight. Hours slid by in Buena Vista Park. We climbed up its terraced sides and wandered around. A weathered tennis net sagged across its court. The grass heaved with deep breaths and whispers. We marveled at streaks of rose and apricot that backlit the fog as the sun went down, and I raked my hands through the colors, smearing the sunset like wet clay. The twinkling lights of the city spoke to me via cosmic braille—and then one of my friends fell into a ditch. We spent a lifetime trying to get her out. Then, one by one, we fell back into the ditch and lay in a rubbery heap, laughing too hard to get up.

My new city charmed me with its grit and soul. And hills. So many hills and steep streets. And tall, old buildings. So unlike the strip malls and brand-new town-size apartment complexes in Orange County. On Sunday mornings, echoes from the drum circles in Alamo Square Park drifted down the hill to my Western Addition studio and mingled with the gospel choirs singing their hearts out at the various Baptist churches in the Fillmore. I made a pot of coffee and stretched on the floor in the middle of the living room, did sit-ups and push-ups, and read the *San Francisco Chronicle*'s Sunday paper starting with the entertainment section, the Pink Pages. I propped up the sports section, which I didn't read, into a paper tent for Nellie to dive under and into.

An elderly retired longshoreman shared a wall with me. Terrance subbed as a janitor at Candlestick Park when his diabetes allowed. Inside his apartment, he wore a hospital boot on his right foot. Terrance shared his fortified wine with me, telling me how the community in Atlanta, where he grew up, had migrated to the Bay Area in the 1940s and 1950s. There were thousands of jobs open to African Americans at the Port of Oakland, and they built a community in the Western Addition full of Baptist churches, soul food restaurants, barbershops, and BBQ joints. Our neighborhood, El Bethel, was a tiny corner of the Western Addition. Terrance told me how the Fillmore, the neighborhood a few blocks west of us, had been the jazz mecca of the West Coast, a Black cultural center that rivaled Harlem. I told him about my family and what I knew about NASA and Cocoa Beach, Florida, where I had grown up, over dinner together at least once a week. A cast-iron skillet full of meat drippings and hardened fat sat on his stove. Terrance would light the gas flame and drop in a couple of pork chops. I brought the beer and made rice with stewed tomatoes and peppers.

A job waited for me here: I had transferred from McCormick & Schmick's in Irvine to McCormick &

Kuleto's in Ghirardelli Square. My studio was two and a half miles away. The bus schedules confused me and I was too proud to ask strangers how the routes and transfers worked, so I walked to and from the restaurant. Plus it seemed naive to expose my wad of tips just to extract eighty-five cents for the bus. I hoofed over Fillmore Street to Eddy, past Planned Parenthood at Van Ness (where I got my birth control pills and health care) and hung a left. I passed Tommy's Joynt, the retro Barbary Coast Hofbrau, House of Prime Rib (an old-fashioned steak and martini restaurant), the BMW and Mercedes dealerships housed in two- and three-story gold-corniced buildings from the 1940s, and mysterious men's bathhouses. So many businesses along Van Ness looked old and sooty—nothing like the new, manicured Southern California suburbs I had recently left.

My starched and ironed work shirt was wrinkled by the time I arrived and soaked through with sweat. My hair was mushroomed into a frizzy mess from the fog. I felt frumpy beneath the blown-glass sea-creature chandeliers that lit McCormick & Kuleto's view of Aquatic Park, the Golden Gate Bridge, and Alcatraz.

I rationed my buffer money from the Irvine ATM haul, and that provided me with time to develop my art. Committed to no specific medium yet, I tried different things to see where my talent took me. I could sing. I painted. I thought a writer might even be tucked inside. Whatever came with ease, I went in that direction. At night, after work, and with a few drinks and a pack of smokes at the ready, I let rip whatever had been trapped inside. Alcohol flamed the fire in my belly and nasty thoughts turned poetic and singed the pages of my journal.

> *Fearless of curdling and speeding tickets*
> *I tear out at ninety miles an hour and crash*
> *I have to get some sleep so I'll be good for later*
> *And that blessed candle will make me dream*
> *once I quelch its flame with bodily fluids*

My apartment made me proud. I painted the furniture, wrapped ugly cables in pretty scarves purchased at thrift stores, and painted a few canvases to decorate the white walls. I sat cross-legged on the floor of my lovely new living room and fidgeted. Now what? Loneliness tugged at me, and I had too many ideas to focus well. The minute I felt a pang of self-pity—I had not made many friends yet, and my soon-to-be ex-husband had not loved me enough to fight for me to stay—I'd leave my perfect apartment. I visited thrift stores, wandered the aisles of the nearby Safeway, smoked outside of bars listening to live music by bands I did not yet know and wasn't willing to pay for. *Only bores and losers feel sorry for themselves.* I thought my calloused attitude made me tough and sexy.

    Half a bottle of Jim Beam gave me the confidence to venture to The Stone, a rock club in North Beach where Chris Whitley was performing. I got there early and shivered in the cavernous, dank club, its black walls and exposed pipes adorned by the scaffolding and can lights above the stage. The stark setting for a mystical and bluesy singer-songwriter like Whitley worked well because Chris burned like wildfire. Slick and sweaty, hollow-cheeked and naked from the waist up except for his guitar strap and cigarette, he smoked while he played guitar and sang. He smiled down on me with the benevolence of Jim Morrison portrayed by Val Kilmer. I wanted to be seen, no longer a wifey tucked under a wing. *Look at me, look at me, I'm a cosmic event blowing up at your feet, Chris Whitley!* Exhilarated by my boldness, I stared at him and did not give a good goddamn what anyone thought. He smiled at me. *I win! I win! I'm anonymous, beautiful, youngish, and free to slither home with whoever, whenever I want.* Not ready to do much else than smile, I went home alone that night and drank myself to sleep.

I drank every night. Most often that led to writing, or at least a good night's sleep. But sometimes not. Sorrow snaked through my dreams and dampened my morning. Sad, I held my knees to my chest and rocked back and forth on the apartment's brown carpet. But more than I cried, I worried. I told myself that if I kept writing and singing, I'd meet the right people. My path was moonlit, and I'd be all right. Anxiety gave way to excitement and got me into the shower and out the door.

A leftover habit from growing up in Florida and living in Southern California sent me outside to deepen my tan. Looking good mattered more than being warm. On my days off, when the temperature hit 65 degrees or higher, I climbed to the top of my apartment building with a six-pack and some Parliament Lights to read *Tales of the City* by Armistead Maupin. I treated those bawdy stories like anthropological studies. That's what I wanted San Francisco to do to me: set my uptight, provincial ass free. Interesting, indented patterns covered the bottoms of my bare feet from walking across the gravel-studded asphalt roofing. I shivered and sunbathed topless under a wide-open sky, reckless and daring, giving myself a hard-on.

Chloe took me to Baker Beach, where we strolled around in bikini bottoms, no tops. Feeling the ocean breeze and imagined eyes on my naked torso felt wild. My hair blew back and I tried not to stare at Chloe's perfect breasts. She could drink a pot of black tea, eat an entire loaf of sourdough with gooey triple-cream brie from the cheese shop on Divisadero (a block from Saint John Coltrane Church), and still look good naked.

I reread Kerouac and Ferlinghetti even though I didn't like them all that much. Most of the Beats were all style, no substance. To me, being cool, man, equaled being cold. Except for Ginsberg. Ginsberg held heat. And Burroughs—I related to something in the creases of his thinking, and his eerie vanity tangled with my own. I did not have the gene that let me enjoy the Grateful Dead. Death was sexy, but the Dead were not. Hippies were lazy and stank. I nonetheless tried to get familiar with some of the more famous artists from San Francisco. I needed the vocabulary. I wanted to be ready, locked and loaded, with information about the place I wanted to belong to. I drank Irish coffee at Vesuvio, then went across the street to City

Lights and reread *Howl*. I felt like a poser but had a hunch that, over time, I would emulate the prostrated destructiveness that Ginsberg's *Howl* extolled.

In the curve of the bay window, legs sprawled on my scratchy brown carpet, I let Leonard Cohen teach me about songwriting. The lyrics "swollen appetite" leapt from the Panasonic boombox speakers as the song "Joan of Arc" played. Those words gripped my fascination with my hollowed-out insides like clothespins. I had a galaxy of unfulfilled longing, and my desire had a slippery tail. Damn, how I wanted to write like Cohen! Make a stranger cry in recognition. Overcome, I masturbated, because art and sex intertwined so naturally that to try to separate them would break the chain and shatter the spell. Words crawled up from the depths onto the page, a gift from Leonard. Not a song exactly, but something interesting, and for a moment, I was satisfied.

The job in Ghirardelli Square lasted all of six weeks before I gave up and gave notice. The challenge to get there, the long shifts, and the lack of potential friend material among my coworkers added up to something too familiar, too Orange County. It was just another upscale restaurant with high check averages but a sterile atmosphere. I missed the nightclub scene and the comics from the Improv days. So when Tommy, a friend from San Diego who'd moved to San Francisco several months before me, said he could get me a job at the legendary Warfield on Market Street, I lunged at the chance. To work with him and all those bands and the stage crew seemed as good an education as finishing the last four credits I still needed for my poly-sci bachelor's degree. I bleached my hair from tasteful blonde to science-experiment platinum. I became a free operator in a place where no one knew me. Ready for my edges to get roughened up, I waded knee-deep into badass coworkers.

Not owning a car toughened me up in another way. The muscles in my legs hardened as I learned about the city on foot. I saw things I'd missed moving at seventy miles per hour along the SoCal freeways: rats in the rosebushes, eye contact, people sleeping in doorways. Sewage wafting up through the grates at street corners. The sidewalks buckling and cracking from giant tree roots. I absorbed their slow-moving disruption that rivaled the flamboyance of earthquakes. I stood hedge-level with the magnificent landscaping in front of the fancier Victorians. The city and I became joined at the hip.

I had a secret crush on Tommy. His presence in San Francisco had added to the allure of moving north. A longtime friend of Brad's, Tommy introduced me to people at the Warfield who, like me, had moved from San Diego to SF to pursue creativity. On his motorcycle, my arms around his waist, we rounded curves on twisty roads above the Golden Gate Bridge. The view from above the Presidio made me hold on tighter, and the buttery smell of Tommy's neck was tempting. I wanted to burrow in and gorge myself. The thought of hurting Brad did not restrain me as much as the thought of how awful it would be if Tommy turned me down. Since I lacked courage, I pined, my unfed desires swollen, just like Cohen said.

Chapter 2 - I Love You. Who Is This?

My shifts at the Warfield began in the first week of May 1992. Outside the venue, on seedy Market Street, the San Francisco police marched in riot gear, anticipating trouble provoked by the one-year anniversary of the not-guilty verdict given to the LAPD caught on video beating Rodney King. Bob Dylan had brought his Never Ending Tour to San Francisco for two nights. Without a sonic reason, the band had two drummers. I would sneak peeks at the fragile state of race relations through the front glass of the two-thousand-seat music venue built in the 1920s, then hustle back to the kitchen to make nachos. I vacillated between freakout and outrage.

More often than not, the musicians performing at the Warfield in the early 1990s were acts I admired: Sonic Youth, the Beastie Boys, Tori Amos, Pearl Jam, Nick Cave. The Henry Rollins Band segued into Henry Rollins's one-man show. Leonard Cohen toured with the *Future* album. The Cocteau Twins tried to keep a toehold even though Elizabeth Frazer was so pregnant she looked like a fertility goddess, the very opposite of scrawny PJ Harvey, who spat nails out of her tiny throat and guitar on the *Dry* tour. Of course, I pretended to be indifferent to some acts— *Hey, I just work here, man, I don't book the shows.* I kept my admiration for Lisa Stansfield, Seal, and Simply Red to myself.

Dwight Yoakam played several nights in a row and filmed a documentary for his biggest-selling album, *This Time*, during my shifts. Spinal Tap had an extensive stage show, and I watched the crew secure air harnesses from the rafters. Close proximity to the musicians, watching the sound checks while I set up tables and chairs, or even just opening industrial-size cans of salsa and refried beans for the nachos, seemed badass, a form of solidarity because we needed each other—the musicians and us house employees. In the circles that mattered most to me, working at the Warfield commanded respect.

The friends I met through Tommy shared my gripes: that the suburbs (where we came from) were lame, that yuppies (who our parents hoped we'd become) sucked, that the mainstream media (not worth the hoop-jumping to get a job with) gave ink to sellouts. We did not need to be model thin or get boob jobs like Los Angeles required, nor well-trained, ambitious, and on a trajectory like what we thought New York expected. San Francisco provided us weirdos with a nesting ground and an unspoken mutual agreement: strive to be unconventional, and don't do it for the money. Become legendary, not famous.

I kept my ambition to myself. I wanted to make money and I really wanted to be famous. I did not need to reinvent the wheel. To be a career waiter in San Francisco held no shame, but I hoped my imagined future band would break sooner than later, or my first novel would be adapted for the silver screen. My arty friends seemed so much more at ease being broke and dirty. It bothered me that some of the artist types I met made inaccessible art for the sake of making art inaccessible. Blech.

I had high hopes but minimal training: a beginner's painting and anatomy class at Costa Mesa Community College and comparative lit classes at San Diego State. A few original paintings hung on my walls, and I'd started several short stories but never finished them. I had sung in the Baptist church choir in Florida and with garage bands during high school in Tennessee. Voted "Most Talented" in high school, with a picture in the yearbook to prove it, I performed shows with my various bands at school functions. It took moving to San Francisco to realize just how many talented people populated the Earth.

Some of my new coworkers at the Warfield had been living in San Francisco for years. They got by on very little money, were active in one art scene or another, and could make a Mission burrito last for two meals. They turned me on to the want ads in the *Bay Guardian* and *SF Weekly* newspapers and told me to always get a bus transfer whether I needed it or not. You can always give it away. Crucially, they taught me how to read the Muni and BART schedules. At the end of our work shifts, we'd pile into the bed of Tommy's ancient International Jeep–like truck, which did not have seat belts—or seats, for that matter—and head over to one of our apartments after a liquor stop. We rode open-air through the sleeping city. Cigarette smoke, unleaded gas, and cucumber lotion scented the fog as we passed old apartment buildings towering on both sides of the streets. I could touch the city at night. A slow-breathing landscape of Art Deco and Art Nouveau, Edwardian and Victorian, slid by like a silent movie.

    I had my first friend crush on Linden, the poet. She had a stick-straight, white-blonde bob and wore MAC Viva Glam matte lipstick and face powder, no eye makeup. Lithe Linden had alabaster skin and blue veins. She managed to look chic in shitty cutoff pants—not cutoff jeans, just shitty cutoff used men's suit pants—with combat boots and black knee-high socks. She introduced me to the ironic T-shirt: always used, and probably a boy's size. You could see her black lace bra under the stretched-to-almost-ripping cotton. She wore a tattered, oversize black leather motorcycle jacket and a knit beanie when it was cold and foggy. I thought she was more glamorous than any tan person I'd ever seen. I found it odd that she didn't let me read her poetry.

    Linden lived in an apartment she shared with a twenty-five-year-old roommate in Albion Alley in the Mission, across from a funeral home. A twenty-nine-year-old woman is ancient compared to a twenty-five-year-old man, or so I thought. I kept my distance. Their place was filthy. Neither Linden nor her roommate cleaned, and I doubt they owned a vacuum. The garbage overflowed in the kitchen—beer cans, used cat litter, and aluminum foil burrito wrappers. I came to find out that a lot of people who rented in San Francisco didn't care about silverware, toilet paper, or hand towels. Not essential to the artist lifestyle, I supposed. I kept my apartment well stocked and spotless. I had trouble thinking or working on art if something needed cleaning.

Linden's boyfriend, Jackie, was renowned in poetry circles. Big and handsome, sometimes shoeless, often scraped up with a black eye or on crutches, he lived on the edge, borderline homeless. But Linden adored Jackie and his poetry. Even though she didn't let him live with her, she was his champion. She said, "There are worse things in life than being an alcoholic." I chewed on that statement.

Most of my time was spent in the Mission or the Lower Haight. Mission burritos were a daily staple, as were drinks at Dalva and the Albion Bar, both on the same block next to the Roxie movie theater and Truly Mediterranean falafel shop. Early one evening, a woman backed into the Albion, holding the door open with her naked rump. Illuminated by the setting sun, an impressive stream of urine hit the bar floor. Shrieks of her laughter shut down the bar chatter. No one tried to stop her, and then she was gone. Show over. How could I ever return to the suburbs after seeing something that unhinged, that magnificent?

Linden took me to spoken word shows, also known as poetry readings. San Francisco's revered poetry legacy spun my head around. I respected the old freaks from the Beat generation who showed up dressed head to toe in black and topped in obligatory berets. Not their poetry so much as their devotion to the form. The new generation of spoken-word performers pumped youthful vitality and multiculturalism into the scene at what became nationally known as "poetry slam" as soon as MTV co-opted the form the next year on *The Real World*. Every now and then I mustered the courage (got snockered enough) to read one of my poems. Certain my performance killed, leveled the room, I put those old Beats in their place. Then I went home, and in the middle of my living room floor, got to work.

Shine and Glaze

I don't think with my brain
I think what hawk talons feel
Not quite holding or catching survival
My eyes scattered in mirror shards
a jagged lobby
staring at you staring at me
glancing at closed eyelids taking turns
A different face on a different pillow
I need a lover to bring out my shine and glaze

One night, after a sloppy evening of spoken word and red wine, we went to Taqueria Cancun on Mission Street. The starchy food soaked up the booze and made the next day livable. From the overhead speakers a distorted mariachi version of a Beatles song blared, and all of us drunks sang along in various languages. I'd become a cell in San Francisco's bloodstream. As we got up to leave, I reached for my leather jacket, then realized it was gone. Panicked, I looked around and asked the people sitting nearby if they'd seen it. Nobody had. My fuzzy-warm connection to humankind chilled.

We left. Wasted and crestfallen, we trudged back toward Albion Alley and discussed what might be happening to my missing coat at that very minute. I theorized that a homeless couple was giving it road rash as they ground it into the asphalt under their fucking. We laughed. My skin thickened. Then a beat-up Datsun careened off the street onto the sidewalk in front of us. Somehow, four Mexican dudes had squeezed into that tiny car, and now all four climbed out and came at us. We stopped mid-stride; Linden's boyfriend raised one of his crutches like a rifle. My insides turned to ice water. But the men were smiling. One of them yelled, "Hey pretty lady, we found your coat!" He held it out to me, and the warm fuzzies returned in a rush. I felt blessed among women. I hugged the man and thanked him to no end. They got back into their tiny car and we all waved with enthusiasm as they drove away. So much goodwill! Such a triumph! My lipstick, my apartment keys, and even a few crumpled dollars were still inside my pockets. I tumbled right back in love with The City.

Linden talked a lot about becoming a sex worker. Always cerebral, her interest lay more in sexual empowerment and creative expression than money. We read Susie Bright, Annie Sprinkle, and Camille Paglia, and while we drank bottle after bottle of cheap red wine, Linden told me stories about her friend who took sex-fetish phone calls. One particular fetish stood out: the client needed to hear precise descriptions of bowls in order to ejaculate. The curve of the bowl's lip, the depth, the temperature of the ceramic or metal, adjectives for "white" and "gleam." These details made him splooge, and he paid big bucks for her vocabulary. Another client was into food fucking. Over the phone, Linden's sex-worker friend described the textures of pies and cakes, watermelon, raw chicken skin. Cheesecakes in particular got him off. She narrated what it felt like to thrust one's dick into the firm yet creamy substance. Her stories aroused me as well.

After a couple of months, Linden had saved enough money from working at the Warfield to go to Prague, her dream city. I understood her desire to travel but hated to lose her so soon—we'd been hanging out nonstop. Before she left, we spent a day together at Osento, a lesbian bathhouse on Valencia Street. Linden flirted and teased, let her fabulous breasts be admired. My flirting skills were undeveloped, and my breasts were not big enough to float. Nonetheless, we soaked up attention in the hot tubs. I rode home on the 22 Fillmore bus with a bag of wet towels and a few books Linden gave me resting on my lap. When I got home, I sank down into a corner of the ugly linoleum kitchen floor, between the oven and cabinets, and cried. Then I ate a banana. My dear friend Greg, who had been a fellow waiter from my Irvine Improv days and now stayed with me on a regular basis in San Francisco, always chided me about proper nutrition. I hoped he would visit again soon.

Thank goodness for my budding friendship with Jolisa, another person Tommy had introduced me to. Jolisa was my height, had tousled, waist-length, bark-colored hair, and did not wear makeup or deodorant. She took me under her wing, first in the Warfield kitchen, which she managed, then out into neighborhoods I had yet to explore. She was my first friend to get a tattoo. In 1992, people who got tattoos were prisoners, or sailors who came through North Beach during Fleet Week. Jolisa got a clown tattooed on her armpit and shaved her underarm hair into a funny little goatee on her happy clown's chin. Along with several roommates, she rented a small house out in the foggy avenues across from Golden Gate Park. The pastel-colored houses looked like the little boxes on the hillsides from the song of the same name, spread out row after row south toward the airport. She and her roommates watched reruns of *Full House*, *The Golden Girls*, and *Howard Stern*. Their aesthetic: lowbrow. Alumni of UCSD, these folks smoked a lot of weed and drank a lot of beer. They glued together empty beer cans to make a room divider that separated the living room into two bedrooms. I took a hit off their bong one night and remembered how much I hated pot. It made me paranoid, and if I was drunk when I smoked, I threw up. I vowed never to hit that bong again.

I worked at the Warfield five or six nights a week and hung out with my coworker friends on and off the clock. We sat on the floor in the horoscope section of Green Apple Books, nestled between Chinese restaurants on Clement Street, and studied Chinese astrology.

"I am the water rabbit," I whispered.

Jolisa looked up from her book and said, "Wood snake," and pointed at herself.

She researched Tommy's sign to see if they were compatible. She'd been in love with Tommy since the day he started working at the Warfield. She loved him so much, she looked like she might cry. Another reason not to act on my Tommy crush.

A depressive Pisces just like my mother, Jolisa let me cook for her, and, just like with my mother, I tried to lift her heavy spirits. We hiked up the trails above the Sutro Baths and beyond Land's End late at night and practiced girly witchy magic, which consisted of drinking beer, burning a Duraflame log piled high with dried tree branches, writing notes to the goddesses, and burning them, their smoke the magic needed to make the requests come true. I wished for a boyfriend and provocative poems. Jolisa wished for Tommy to fall in love with her. The lights on the Golden Gate Bridge twinkled and reflected red off the eyes of a family of raccoons at the firelit periphery.

Jolisa and I wanted to open a coffee shop in China Basin, a scruffy industrial neighborhood near the port where the Giants would build their ballpark a decade later. Coffee was starting to be a big deal, and Muddy Waters was the only game in town. At our much-cooler-than-Muddy-Waters coffee shop, we'd display our friends' paintings, host spoken word, and have live acoustic music. I planned the menu. I came up with muffin and tart recipes, and we held tastings at my apartment. Onion and fennel tarts and corn and tomato parmesan muffins became my signature dishes. We were serious enough to take a "How to Open a Cafe" class at the Learning Annex, which held classes at the Cathedral Hill Hotel behind Tommy's Joynt on Van Ness. I even typed out our small-business proposition on my electric Brother typewriter, and Jolisa submitted it to City Hall. But raising the required money challenged us to the point of dropping the whole idea. I had trouble paying my own rent.

I eased into city living, went to more shows, met more friends, and shopped at thrift stores even though they smelled like chicken bouillon and melted crayons. I wriggled out of my suburban skin into my city skin. I cultivated a look: not quite rockabilly, not quite grunge, not quite San Diego aerobics teacher. In my fabulous apartment, I always had a bottle of something red or brown by my side, a pack of smokes, and my boombox at the ready for an impromptu mixtape session or a new poem that begged to be recorded. Wax and burn spots dotted my cat's fur from slinking too close to lit candles—the same candles I found still burning in the morning because I had passed out and forgotten to extinguish them.

My ex-sister-in-law, Gina, visited me once right after I moved to The City. I was hopeful our relationship would survive the divorce. Gina was feminine and kind, and cool for a suburban housewife. She reminded me of Stevie Nicks in the 1970s. She and I went to the Castro to get various parts of our bodies pierced—her nose, my belly button. We spoke by phone often, and about six months after I'd moved to San Francisco, she put her daughter on the phone. My three-year-old niece asked me if my hair was pulled up in a ponytail or down.

"It's pulled up," I replied. "Is your hair in a ponytail?"

"No, it's down," she replied.

"It looks pretty down, but feels good pulled up when it's hot," I said.

She said she gets juice when it's hot. We sang "You Are My Sunshine" over the phone. Then she said, "I love you. Who is this?"

One of the tenants in my apartment building kept pulling the fire alarm in the middle of the night. Turns out the man was dying from AIDS and using crystal meth to cope. A meth psychotic. Since I got home from work late at night, I was awake. I waited at the window, bleary and blotto at two or three in the morning, as I watched the fire engine pull up to the curb, its red lights bouncing off the Victorian windows across the street. After a few minutes, a firefighter would knock on my door as they made their mandatory door-to-door check of each apartment.

One night at the Warfield, one of my favorite bands, Paul Kelly and the Messengers, headlined. Their song "Stories of Me," along with Nick Cave's "I'll Love You Until the End of the World," were my go-to songs while drinking a few nightcaps. On this particular night, I must have had a few too many on-the-job drinks. I yelled out from the floor in my tough cocktail-server voice, "Hey Paul! Play 'Stories of Me'!"

Paul Kelly replied from the stage, "We already played that."

His comment got under my skin. I couldn't decide if that made me cool or not, to be that buzzed at work. From that point on, it nagged at me to listen to Paul Kelly.

The perks the Warfield job offered made it worth sticking around, even if we didn't make much money. We drank for free, ate anything we wanted, got to watch our favorite bands, and smoked while we worked. We handwrote our bar tickets, which made stealing easy to get away with. Too guilt-ridden to be a truly good thief, I still tucked a few extra bucks that weren't mine into my pocket. Even so, I needed to find another part-time job.

Hungover most mornings, I chided myself over coffee: go to bed earlier, drink water between drinks, try to write sober. Work on art during the day and work for money at night. I was almost thirty and needed to buckle down and get shit done. But by the time I got home from work each night, my resolve vanished.

Planted cross-legged on the floor of my apartment, surrounded by candles, on any given night I was ready to receive the night gifts. I waited for this all the damn day—even if I was out with friends, I couldn't wait to get home to write. Caramelized grain cleared my sinuses before I tasted the Jim Beam. God's eyes were elsewhere. Brad couldn't judge me, my mother couldn't criticize me, and my sister and brothers would not overhear my attempts. Fire slid down my throat and warmed my belly. In this time and place, creativity grew mossy. This euphoric moment mattered more than any tomorrow. A soft-lead pencil wrote lyrics all on its own. I became infatuated with the sound of my own voice on replay in the headphones, my own candlelit reflection in the uncurtained bay window or bathroom mirror. I took erotic pictures of myself with my Instamatic 110mm film camera. My nipples could cut glass, my heart thudded between my slick thighs. No flower more fragrant, no animal more made of meat, no skin more taut.

Dear Venus,
Send me a man.

Chapter 3 - His Voice Rising from My Throat

Before I left Brad and moved to San Francisco, I fell in love with a country singer. When not at work at the Irvine Improv, Brad and I interned for the distributor of Warner Records. They sent boxes of promotional CDs and posters, which we took to record stores in Orange and San Diego Counties, where we built displays, decorated endcaps, and provided other promotional services. It was Brad's gig, but I tagged along.

In one of those boxes, I found a CD by a new alternative country singer whose music got my attention. At the time I was still a fledgling fan of country music with a limited range of comparison. Other than the cowpunk Lone Justice and The Knitters put out, this recording reminded me of what Elvis Costello did on his country album *Almost Blue*. The country music I listened to came from Emmylou Harris and, by proxy, Gram Parsons. I was familiar with that cosmic country music scene because I'd dated a guy right after high school who worked on the Emmylou Harris tours.

The force of my attraction to the music on the promo CD welded me to some unknown metal. At the time I did not realize I wanted out of my marriage. But the way this guy Charlie sang—it tugged at me, drew me away from Brad and closer to the stereo speakers. I shared the singer's utter heartbrokenness, his sad, sad laments. I had not realized how unhappy I was until his voice told me. I wanted his breath in my hair, his hands on my skin, his voice rising from my throat. His songs tore a hole through the skin that almost didn't hold me together, drunk on that black bottle of Freixenet, rolling around on the floor.

So: Guess who came to town a few months after I landed in San Francisco, single, with a swollen appetite and a cool apartment all my own? Guess who became Charlie's San Francisco girlfriend in the early 1990s?

I had seven days to rev with anticipation before we met. Sitting on the bus, hands covered in ink smudges from rifling through the pages of the *Bay Guardian*, I had almost jumped out of my seat when I discovered that next week, he would open for Mary Chapin Carpenter at Slim's—the jewel of the South of Market nightclub scene, owned by Boz Scaggs. While I revved, I memorized every lyric. My eyes burned holes through the liner notes from staring at the pictures of him on the front and back covers of the CD.

On the big night, I suited up and led the charge of my own goddamn sexual revolution. Armed with a pack of Marlboro Reds and a few poems tucked in the pocket of my vintage black Persian wool coat, I dabbed one precious drop of my almost-empty bottle of Opium perfume behind each earlobe and went to see Charlie Incarnate. My fantasy life had been pretty good but seeing him on stage snapped my idea of good in half. By the time Mary Chapin Carpenter came out, I was also good and sauced. A few minutes into her set, the electricity went out and the nightclub went dark. Undaunted, that woman gave one hell of a show, strutting around the emergency votives set on the bar in her cowboy boots, strumming her acoustic guitar, and singing loud enough for all to hear without the help of the PA. She sparked my bravado, and I snaked my way across the room to the backstage area, Charlie's CD insert at the ready, hoping for more than an autograph.

And there he stood, at the edge of the crowd, benevolent as Jesus in his shoulder-length bi-level, giving himself to his fans. I got an autograph and told him about my poetry. Asked if he'd like me to read a poem to him over a drink across the street at the Paradise Lounge. His bass player, who I found out later was friends with Charlie's fiancée, gave me a dirty look. Not nearly as dirty as the poem I read to Charlie.

We made silly jokes and sketched our family histories. Then the conversation took an intense turn. Over that first drink, I found out that his father (a minister) had cheated on his mother and that he could never forgive him. I told him my father was schizophrenic and that I had been exorcised by the Baptist Church when I was ten. We discovered we had the same birthday, just eight years apart, which implied something kismet about our meeting. Aries battling for control of Mars, and I hoped to lock horns. Emboldened by all this talk, I pulled out the folded pages of promised poems and read a few stanzas. He leaned in to hear me better, and I could smell pot on his breath. It was too loud to continue reading to him, so I handed Charlie the wrinkled pages. He read for a few minutes, whistled under his breath, then looked me in the eye and said, "Damn." I felt seen. He got me. Back at my apartment, he brought his acoustic guitar inside, citing the danger of leaving valuables in a car parked on the street, and I knew he was staying the night. Out of my mind and body with anticipation and vodka, I admired the smeary, candlelit puppet show of our shadows on the wall.

It was serious business, going after a famous stranger and snagging him. I imagined groupies to be carefree lovelies, orbiting the stars of celebrity on gauzy wings. I was anything but carefree and did not consider myself a groupie. We were peers, both of us artists, and I could wave this someday in Brad's face. But more than spite, I wanted to prove to myself that I was somebody, too. Reeling with power and lust, we got together every time Charlie came through the Bay Area.

The affair broke open a mother lode of creativity trapped inside me. I could not stop writing poetry, which I sent off in wine-smeared letters to my new beau. He called me as soon as he received them, flattered and excited to see me again. We spoke on the phone for large swaths of time. That relationship made me resolve to become a country singer myself. But when I told him that plan, his tone changed. He tried to temper my expectations, reminding me how hard it was. Didn't I remember how low the turnout was at his last Bay Area gig? I didn't buy it. Maybe he just didn't want the competition.

My mother had had four children in five years: girl, boy, girl, boy. The two older siblings had coached us younger ones from opposite corners of the living room, all the furniture pushed against the walls to create a boxing ring in the middle. Pitted against my little brother, we skirted each other and threw a few punches, not wanting to inflict real pain—until one of us hit just a little too hard. Then the fight was on and would end in tears.

On the hotel bed or my futon, a nibble on my neck escalated to a nip on the lips, which led to bites that broke the skin and left bruises on the fleshy parts of my body. The pain jolted me awake during drunken sex. I called the swollen bouquet of bite marks that ringed my thighs the purple roses. It scared Charlie—the damage he left on my limbs, and the fact that I asked for it.

I thought his real girlfriend, the one he said he was going to be faithful to by not having intercourse with me, was fragile and needy. With no strings attached, I offered a pound of flesh. Because I felt irresistible, I believed he would lose interest in anyone but me. Yet each visit, he reminded me of the rules (no intercourse), and each visit, I pushed the boundaries. Who knows what happened; we were both wasted.

I turned the purple roses into art. As soon as he left town, I dressed in lingerie, put on makeup, and took photos of myself in fishnets ripped to reveal black, blue, and ruddy-ringed bruises. Evidence that I could live to tell the tale of being eaten alive. I felt beautiful in my abraded skin. I hoped the person who developed the film at Walgreens got as excited as I did when the images revealed themselves. One of my first audiences.

I got to know the doormen at the Phoenix Motel, a funky lodge in the Tenderloin long favored by the touring rock 'n' roll set. I stopped feeling self-conscious about the obvious reason for my visits. Inside Charlie's room, he held up various Nudie jackets and other vintage Western wear and asked my opinion. He took his stage presence seriously, and I loved that he sought my approval. Every single morning, regardless of how late we had partied, he went for a run. I giggled upon waking, awash in decadence from all the fun I was having.

One morning when Charlie had a morning radio promotion to go to, I found myself asking the doorman at the Phoenix to call me a cab when the sun was not yet up. Charlie walked outside as the cab pulled up, and before I got in, we engaged in a very long goodbye kiss. As the ride got under way, the cabbie asked me, "Who was that?" all smarmy-like.

"Oh, that's my brother."

I smiled to myself in the back seat.

Chapter 4 - Two-Drink Minimum

A slew of comedy clubs were thriving in San Francisco in the late 1980s and early 1990s: the Punch Line, Cobb's, Holy City Zoo, the Purple Onion, the Other Café, the Other Other Café. And in 1988, the cable-TV-ready Improv, with its black-and-white checkered tile motif and red brick backdrop, joined the robust scene. Because Brad and I had been on the opening crew, I felt like I had been a midwife at its birth. For the three months we'd spent getting the place up and running, the elevator to the kitchen shared with Jack in the Box had stopped working. I helped out our waiters, running up and down the stairs to retrieve potato skins and fried mozzarella sticks. The day Jack in the Box's plumbing burst and sprayed a fine mist of sewage into the renovated showroom, my clothes were every bit as soiled as Brad's before we got the hell out of that stinky basement.

And so, the fully established San Francisco Improv seemed a logical place for me to augment my Warfield earnings, except that nobody there knew me. I applied for a job anyway, not bolstered by the confidence nepotism brings, but confident; when it came to a two-drink minimum, I knew my shit. I got the job. The staff could not have been nicer or more welcoming to me.

Along with the cocktailing job, I picked up a union-wage job that had just become available cleaning the comedy condominium. Instead of booking hotel rooms for the headliners to stay in during their weeklong runs, the owner leased a condo. I emptied the trash, cleaned the toilet, vacuumed, and changed the sheets. Along with slinging cocktails, the condo-cleaning duties boosted my income a lot.

Some of the comedians I knew from Southern California expressed uncertainty about continuing a friendship with me. And none of them dared touch me with a ten-foot pole, since the good graces of Brad mattered way more than sleeping with me. He'd done very well on the management end of the comedy scene food chain, and his new girlfriend, who just happened to be a comic, had been featured in a recent *Playboy* magazine layout devoted to "Hot Women in Comedy." The local comics tried to be nice, though, and even took pity on me because they assumed Brad had dumped me. *Well, fuck those dummies! They're pony jumpers. I am a poet!* Plus, San Francisco's homegrown comedy scene did not give two shits about Brad. As far as my dating life and the Improv went, my saving grace was that I was more attracted to musicians than comedians any day of the week.

For the record, there is no marketing more important to a comic's career than the word of mouth provided by service-industry employees, which includes cocktail servers, bartenders, and hotel concierges. Case in point: I was sitting one evening at the bar at the Mad Dog in the Fog in the Lower Haight and ordered a frothy black and tan while I waited for Billy, a bartender at the Improv and my new best friend, to join me. The woman sitting on the barstool to my right happened to be a concierge at the Hyatt, and we struck up a conversation. I told her what a hack so-and-so happened to be and how I had three more shifts of his show to endure. She lit my cigarette and said a different so-and-so was at Cobb's. I said I wished she played the Improv but she was just too damn dirty. We laughed. The concierge knew which tourists to direct to which comedy club: she would send the morons to us and the cool people to Cobb's.

San Francisco's comedy scene fostered much wilder roots than what the Improv chain featured. Even though the headliners were big names from all over, the openers and middle acts were most often locals. SF comedians were ribald, unconventional, blue, and truly improvisational. They had an abundance of clubs and stages to work out their acts, and the local audiences were sophisticated. Our particular Improv was small and intimate—a basement art house compared to its monolith sibling clubs in Irvine and Tempe. Local comedians like Patton Oswalt, Blaine Capatch, and Tony Camin hung out with us even when they weren't in the night's lineup. Larry "Bubbles" Brown called us "goddesses," which I appreciated, and we repeated his catchphrase to one another ad nauseam while we worked: "Bitter?" "Just a tad." Tom Rhodes, Greg Proops, and Doug Benson were stoners extraordinaire and loved to go out drinking with us after hours. Even Robin Williams popped up on a regular basis when Debi Durst, Jack Boulware, Geoff Bolt, or the ensemble cast of the National Theatre of the Deranged performed improvisational comedy on Monday nights.

The San Francisco comedians blew what I thought I knew about comedy out my suburban ass. They had new perspectives and took risks. That exposure tore open my own artistic world. I attacked poetry reading the way Matt Weinhold took to the stage, with my arms swinging, leaning into the make-believe audience. I emulated Patton Oswalt's self-mockery and Marc Maron's bold insights into sexuality and mind-fuckery. This led to a new variety of flower blooming in my artistic field: writing sincere yet sexual country songs. Songs I knew I had nailed because they made *me* cry. Those I kept to myself, sat on, and incubated for a later hatch.

An MTV VJ wooed me by whispering dirty stories into my ear, always in public. Told me I was his favorite niece but to pretend we weren't related. Said what he planned to do to me later and perhaps on the roof. His heavy breathing and imagination left me unable to stand. But after several weeks of consistent dating—always thirty-six hours together followed by twenty-four hours apart—I found a note in my apartment that read, "What's missing." For someone with complicated yet steadfast rules (thirty-six on, twenty-four off), he was also naughty and fun, so I thought he'd taken my panties. But when asked, he said, "Love. Love is missing." Yeah, well, that. I loved Charlie. Anybody else was just a placeholder during his absences.

Over the phone a few weeks earlier, Charlie had broken up with me because his fiancée insisted on it. When we first started to see each other, he'd warned me that this might happen. I hadn't believed him. How could she possibly keep his attention after *me*? On that call, I pretended to be cool with the breakup—dignified, even cordial. I acknowledged that he had warned me and said I understood. Then I hung up and threw half a burrito into the garbage as hard as I could. Beans and rice littered my kitchen floor. I ran to the corner store and into the comforting arms of Jim Beam. I told my friends my heart was sprained, not broken, and I dated everyone.

Dear Missteps,
You overwhelm me.
There are too many of you to name, so I won't.

Oh, the San Francisco Improv crew! Billy became my first true and lasting friend from The City. British, androgynous, and incredible under pressure, he looked like a vampire rock star as he towered over the bar in his long black jeans. When he smiled, he transformed from a brooding goth into a charming goth with great manners—perhaps a cast member of the *Rocky Horror Picture Show* London production. He looked like someone who worked as a bartender on a lark because hanging out with Siouxsie Sioux and Peter Murphy had grown tedious. He was also a prolific cartoonist. He lived a few blocks away from me on Oak Street, on the other side of Alamo Square, with his goth wife. Our lifelong friendship began as we walked to work together and talked our heads off the whole way there, throughout the shift, and on the cab ride home.

Mia, another Improv waiter, befriended me. Mia, a cabaret singer. Mia, a cultured woman from the East Coast. Mia, political and educated at Mills College. Mia, whose original music landed on a Wim Wenders soundtrack. Sometimes late at night after all the bars closed and we shared a cab ride home, I goaded her into singing one of her songs, a cappella, for the driver. I pimped her talent. I wanted everyone to know what they were in the presence of. And I basked in her glow. I hoped to someday be as good a singer as Mia, but I knew I had work to do. My list of things to prove grew longer and bothered me somethin' fierce. I needed to drink to get it up or shove it down.

The staff at the Improv slogged through two shows a night during the week and three on Fridays and Saturdays. With its two-drink minimum per person, we slung a lot of booze. Some drank more than two drinks a show. Some who drank more than two drinks each show were not customers. As a crew, we chugged drinks to get through demanding nights. I tried to wait until the second half of the second show before sneaking a shot. A sipped beer in the corner helped prolong the moment before it was time for the hard stuff. We worked the shows and laughed or didn't, depending on whether the comic warranted our esteem. We counted piles of cash at the end of each night and celebrated or groused with tequila and beer. We compared stories about asshole customers and lame tourist tips and gossiped. Some comedians stuck around and hung out with us. In Southern California, we had gossiped about who was a hack, or who was gay and in the closet, or a beard, and so forth. In San Francisco, we gossiped about who left town for Los Angeles or which comics got writer jobs and if they'd sold out. Oh, and who was gay and in the closet.

Once a week I made the steep trek up Taylor Street to the headliner's apartment to clean. The condo building (now the Amsterdam Hostel) loomed on the corner of Taylor and Bush, where the male porn shops and Chinese restaurants ended and Nob Hill began. Most comics were just regular people with regular dirt and didn't leave mangy filth in their wake. But a few could not have cared less what the cleaning woman thought of their piggy ways. And then there was Greg Travis. He and his girlfriend had the flu the week he worked the Improv, and even though I adored his act, especially his character David Sleaze, the Punk Magician, in which he wore a mohawk wig and did a variety of stupid magic tricks with audience participation, they obliterated the condo. Snotty tissues were stuck to everything, including an unspeakable toilet, and picked-over takeout food was left unplated on the arms of the couch and coffee table. On the flip side, they also left half-empty bottles of booze and unsmoked cigarettes.

Because of my friendship with Mia, I became a fan of the band Bongwater. The lead singer, Ann Magnuson, appeared in a one-woman show called *You Could Be Home Now* that played for two weeks at the Alcazar Theatre on Geary in the fall of 1993. For whatever reason, the theater put her up in the Improv's condo. Thrilled, I just couldn't wait to clean up after Ms. Magnuson. After her first week, I hung out in the hallway and waited for her to leave so I could tidy the place. I got there early and tucked into an alcove in the hallway so I could listen to her warm-up singing exercises. Lost in her voice, I floated past layers upon layers of cream-colored paint in the chipped molding. After she left for the show, I went to change the sheets, vacuum, and take out the garbage. On the mantel, I found an almost-empty vial of herbal throat tincture and finished it for her.

One-person comedy shows were a big deal at this time. The very first shift I worked at the SF Improv, Rick Reynolds headlined. He performed his one-man show, *Only the Truth Is Funny*, for three months. I admit the first time I saw his act, I laughed more than a few times. I was still used to being a good sport. But by the end of that run, I could have stabbed myself in the eye with a fork when he got to the "I thought there was one more cookie" bit. And then Jeff Garlin had his one-man show, *I Want Someone to Eat Cheese With*. *Someone to Cut Cheese With* (what we called the show behind Jeff's back) ran way too long and was only tolerable because smart and funny-cool girl Janeane Garofalo opened. The longest-running one-person show was Rob Becker's *Defending the Caveman*. These kinds of shows made tourists feel like they were getting a dose of big-city culture. Hearing the clichéd differences between men and women, over and over again, for months, gave the waitstaff a good reason to drink on the job.

On the weekends, after the third and last show of the night, we'd lock up the Improv and head across Geary to the Wine Bar for more after-hours drinking in the walk-in vault at the back. I envisioned flocks of club and restaurant workers mid-flight throughout the city, alighting upon various tree branches. A typical night after work landed us in the Lower Haight. Always handy, it was walking distance from most of our apartments. If a fistfight broke out at Casa Loma, we ducked out fast and went across the street to the Mad Dog, where Brits filled the tables and the World Cup played on their one television screen, back before soccer got big in the States. If that was too packed and rowdy, we trotted down to the end of the block to the MidTown, where they served real drinks—cocktails, as opposed to just cider or beer. We'd play pool while the Smashing Pumpkins droned through the speakers, and I'd buy a pack of disgusting Camels because the cigarette machine had run out of Marlboros. I lit each next cigarette on the cherry of the last until the pack ran out.

One night after work, our crew went to an after-show party at a rich person's house in Pacific Heights. The three-story mansion scaled the side of a hill and had a sweeping view of the Marina. I had seen monoliths of wealth like this through the window of the 22 Fillmore bus. Inside, the house was packed with comics and club workers. Lonesome and armed with opinions I'd take to the mat, I prowled for someone to tangle with. At the tail end of the party, I sat across the dining room table from an up-and-coming star. His comedy act contained a lot of sex commentary. He was a dirty, dirty bird, and I wanted to know him better.

"You know who you remind me of?" I asked.

"No. Who?" the dirty bird said.

"Bill Hicks. Well, more precisely, Bill Hicks lite."

My come-on came out sideways. This guy looked like he might take a swing at me, then just walked away.

He knew how to handle mean drunks. A few years later, he moved to Los Angeles, and my ex-husband, Brad, became his manager.

Thank goodness I could go straight home, straight to the comforting voice of Nick Cave. I needed him to sing to me, and only me.

Making mixtapes was like practicing the rosary. One song after another, a reckoning followed by a sonic epiphany that rolled between numb fingertips. I tried hard not to pass out before I finished placing the perfect song in the perfect order on the cassette. I recorded myself slurring an original poem, then I'd echo its sentiment with a song. I couldn't wait to give these tapes to Linden, Billy, my sister, whoever I was dating. Even to Charlie, when I wanted him to remember what he had lost by ending our relationship.

As I listened back to these creations on my Panasonic boombox, I wobbled in the middle of a semicircle of candles melting onto Goodwill teacup saucers, a cigarette cherry burning holes into the first two fingers of my right hand. So brave to be on my own and so lost in the vastness of my desire.

Chapter 5 - Journal Entry, October 5, 1992

I'm starting to live on less. Less sleep, less money, less interaction through obligation with others. More time, though.

The insomnia is back. Can't figure it out. Last week it distressed me to the point of contemplating suicide. When I'm tossing and turning, back aching, cheek wrinkling, leg asleep but not brain, everything crosses my mind.

I see a pattern. The last time I had trouble sleeping was before Charlie was due. He unsettles me. But after our good talk yesterday and after the sense of relief I recognized at work—we will be friends. Put love on the back burner of his real girlfriend's stove.

I still wasn't able to do more than 2:30 'til 6:55. I've decided to watch the sunrise from the rooftop instead of fuming. It's the first one I've ever seen blaze over the East Bay and make a silhouette of the Civic Center dome. Very quiet, the sunrise—I can't decide if it is full of a radiant promise or menacing stealth—each delivers day after day after day…

Swollen Appetite

  Today I am going to have breakfast with Linden then we go to the bathhouse. Perfect. She's teetering on au revoir. Tomorrow is the airport and then Prague. It feels very quiet, her exit, this morning and my love for Charlie.
  The Baptists haven't come out yet. I don't usually see them arrive. Usually I don't see them until after the services when I'm getting coffee and a paper. I wonder if the preachers are rehearsing or just having coffee (is that allowed?) or musing through the paper, getting material to juxtapose w/ the Bible at showtime? I'm sure there are some good clergy. By 10 am Golden Gate's three lanes will be reduced to one straight and narrow, smack-dab down the middle of the double-parked.

Sunday, 11:30 pm
I've been hitting more highs and lows than ever before. They seem to feed off each other. It's wearing me out in a different way than mediocracy did.
  Middlin' is easy to sustain. But none of it feels controllable.
  I like not being the driver.
  Work at the Improv was slow, yeah. I was trying to keep the tears for later and making myself laugh at stupid jokes for distraction. Now I'm home again. Glad to be on my own for now. Nellie's so passionate, makes me feel special.
  We are married.

Sandra Austin Mello

Chapter 6 - You're Just Getting Started

Music had been my saving grace since childhood. It swept worried thoughts away like a broom whisking dirt off the porch, leaving the wood smooth. A clean start. The family life I experienced as a kid lurched from one mental health crisis to the next, and music stopped me from thinking about how bad my head hurt. How my heart was bleeding out. At the age of sixteen, I also discovered the comforting effects of alcohol and my life got better.

> Dear music and alcohol,
> You saved my life. Thank you.
> AMEN.

In the early 1980s, while New Wave gushed over the airwaves and dance floors, I worked at Record City, an independent music store on Colonial Drive in Orlando. The import section we called Punk / Nouveau Vague because some of the people in charge of the displays were musical snoots. Working there seemed like boot camp for an army of cool. They beat the livin' Kansas and Heart out of my record collection. They smirked when I bragged about seeing Rush twice on the *Moving Pictures* tour. It only took a whiff of ridicule to make me disloyal to what had kept me sane during my high school years in rural Tennessee. So long, Foreigner! Get lost, Styx. Take a hike, you stupid dummy Scorpions. My coworkers introduced me to *Melody Maker* and *Creem* magazines and LA fanzines. To me, the fanzines looked kind of shitty and unprofessional, but I was missing the point. I learned about bands I had no prior exposure to, like The Blasters, Roxy Music, X, The Jam. Thank fucking god I didn't show up a few years later in Southern California still playing Pat Benatar and April Wine!

In the mid-to-late 1980s, my soon-to-be ex-husband Brad and I forged our relationship and bonded over our mutual love of David Bowie. He had exceptional taste in music, and we went to scads of live shows: The Pixies, Jane's Addiction, Drivin' and Cryin', Robyn Hitchcock, Lloyd Cole, Dream Syndicate, Matthew Sweet, Concrete Blonde, REM, and the Throwing Muses, to name a few. But deep inside I felt like a cheat, both for not finding new music on my own, not since Record City anyway, and for not trusting my own taste unless it was corroborated. Basically, I liked what you liked more than what I liked. A reed in the river. And yet, despite my chameleon-esque qualities, there was a trinity of musicians that, under no circumstances, did I forsake:

God the Father was David Bowie. The musical divinity at whose feet I fell and showed my belly. His music and persona gave me a taste for grandeur and baritones. He lit the swinging bridge that hung in tatters under my unacknowledged spirit, and when I looked up, glitter anointed me. I dreamed about Bowie throughout my young adulthood and I was hot for Daddy, but Daddy was too good to have sex with me. Oh, how I suffered. I had more erotic dreams about Bowie than any other musician. Well, anyone other than Emmylou Harris.

Emmylou Harris was my Jesus. Beatific, she saved me time and time again. When sorrowful, Emmylou embraced me in protective bands of vibrato. I went to her for restoration, consolation, to be lifted up. Just like any savior worth their salt, she showed me the way.

Leonard Cohen, my holiest of Ghosts. He spoke in tongues of poetry and fire. As stark as the Buddha, if the Buddha wore a fedora. Who else could feature a cheesy electric piano on a third of their recordings and still inspire? Leonard understood humanity, even liked us, deeming us lovely and worth entertaining. Cohen bucked my spirit and infused me with the desire to write. He encouraged my deepest suspicion: that sex is holy.

So in the early 1990s in San Francisco, I finally sought to discover what pleased me most. I could not afford to go out and buy a record at full retail. I could not follow the expensive mainstream. Instead, I rummaged through the cutout bins in the back-right corner of Recycled Records. Also Reckless Records and Amoeba, when they came along. Insights from the music reviewers in the *Bay Guardian* and the *SF Weekly*—Denise Sullivan, Sylvie Simmons, Gina Arnold, Neva Chonin, Tommy Tompkins, Johnny Ray Huston, John O'Neill—guided me at the bins and to the clubs for live shows. Intriguing album art and poetic song titles could also separate me from a dollar or two. Buying cutouts did not gouge my yellow-rice-and-Hamm's-beer budget too much.

Hungover, insecure, and defensive, I searched for something new and exciting yet priced to move. The click of the plastic covers hitting one another was already a song in and of itself. One of the first CDs I took home and listened to was the *Acoustic Music Project: A Benefit for Project Open Hand*, which had been recorded live at the Great American Music Hall in 1991. For the first time I heard a dozen or so San Francisco–based singer-songwriters, and that recording became a primer of sorts that introduced me to local songwriting royalty, in particular Mark Eitzel, whom I would soon follow in American Music Club, Jill Olson from the pop band the Movie Stars and the country band Red Meat, and the duo Chuck Prophet and Stephanie Finch. I wanted to sound like me, but I also hoped that that was just like Stephanie. Her honey voice highlighted Chuck's baritone and drove me to find my own Chuck.

One magical day, I splurged. I walked through the doors of Rough Trade Records on Haight Street. Possessed by the gall a few afternoon drinks provided, I faced the cool people inside—people who scared me because I had stealth cool and they had apparent cool. I did not make eye contact. I browsed through the two parallel aisles down the middle of the store, nonchalantly flipping through rows of molded plastic. And there I discovered the CD that changed my life: *Miss America* by Mary Margaret O'Hara. No one recommended *Miss America*, but the titles of the songs matched the scars on my psyche: "To Cry About," "Body's in Trouble," "Not Be Alright," "You Will Be Loved Again." I forked over a whopping $13.49.

I could not stop listening to this CD. Mary purred, she groveled, she stumbled, she threw words at the walls and then picked them up gently and cooed over them. A connection this feral I had not been infected by since the 1980s, when I listened to Rickie Lee Jones's *The Magazine*. A sister in distress, Mary Margaret sounded downright off her meds at times on the song "Year in Song," with the words, "Is the aim eh joy?" Over and over Mary Margaret O'Hara splattered that question on my mirror. I hurt, I endured, I felt murderously misunderstood, and above all else, I waded in loneliness. And then she acknowledged a body in trouble and asked, "Who do you talk to? Who?" During that song, the sweat from the previous exorcism dried. I curled up and sucked my thumb, my poor, poor, pour-me-another-drink thumb, while she begged to know from the one who'd left her why he ran away. She held onto his pant leg and seduced him into coming back with her beautiful voice in the song "Dear Darling." This woman expressed what I wanted to express with such musical acuity, it inspired me to let loose even more. I had a big, beautiful voice I did not know how to use. In a neurotic alliance with Mary, we raced the demons. She whispered into my ear, *You're just getting started.*

Chapter 7 - 28 White Doves

A strong sex drive in the early 1990s could turn into a death sentence. Gay or straight, we all knew someone dying from AIDS. My straight friends and I told one another that we were serious about not becoming infected and recognized how scary it was, especially for our gay friends. We lived at its epicenter, after all. Yet it was rare for me to ask my partners to wear condoms, maybe because I became sexually active when birth control pills were readily available in the years prior to HIV. Or maybe because they never had one at the ready, nor did I, and I didn't want to interrupt the sexual momentum. And more often than not, I didn't ask because I was shitfaced.

My circle of friends in The City did minor drugs like weed and cocaine, but at the edges of that circle, I knew folks who shot heroin. Sometimes those people shared needles. Or had sex with someone who shared needles. Or had had sex with someone infected and didn't get tested. I held my breath, said I had recently been tested, and went ahead and had unprotected sex.

Even though Charlie owned my heart, that did not stop me from taking pleasure when I needed it and he wasn't handy. Not long after I started at the Warfield, I dated a tall bartender from a cool local indie-rock band. He and I went to the county health department and were tested for AIDS together, as a couple. After that relationship ended, I lied to my next partner about being tested. And then the next. Too much poor judgment flowed under that precarious bridge and, frightened, I decided, *What's the use?*

In five years of mostly unprotected sex, I got tested once.

My buddy Greg and I had worked together as servers at the Irvine Improv. One evening he was standing next to me while I arranged a carafe of rosé and four empty glasses in the center of my cocktail tray and eight shots of Jägermeister around the edge. Greg drummed his fingers on the bar. "Pick up the pace, sister! We haven't got all day." He analyzed the contents of my tray. "You got the sophisticated bachelorette party, I see." Then he sniffed at the rosé. "Visitors from La Brea to boot." He winked and hustled me along so he could fill his own cocktail tray. His playful dishing made me laugh and made work fly by, and we became fast friends. He was unaware then that HIV had already begun chewing away at his immune system.

Greg resembled a willowy Steve McQueen: tan, with pale blue eyes, fawn-colored hair, and a slow smile. Charming and quick-witted, he was playful until one too many drinks slid down his throat. Then his humor left bite marks. Not long before I separated from Brad, Greg landed a good job at the corporate offices for Toyota in Long Beach. Toyota threw an extravagant Christmas party in Studio City, and Greg asked me to be his date. I wore my nicest black dress and heels, swung a vintage clutch that held just my smokes and lipstick, and Greg introduced me as his fiancée to his homophobic boss. I took classes at nearby Long Beach State University and spent time at his apartment before and after classes, eating takeout and drinking beers, before going home to Brad in Irvine.

Then I didn't hear from him for a few months and got worried. I tracked him down, and he told me he had tested positive for HIV. He'd cashed in his life insurance, quit his good job, and moved back in with his parents in San Jose. At the beginning of our friendship, he had told me the story of the very first time he had sex with a man, how it was shameful, rushed, in a bathroom, and unprotected. After coming out, he always used protection, since AIDS stalked his friends and no one knew exactly how it spread. Greg could very well have contracted HIV from that miserable first sexual encounter.

After I moved to San Francisco, Greg spent plenty of time in The City with me. We volunteered twice a week at Project Open Hand, a nonprofit that delivered warm meals to the growing number of local people with HIV/AIDS. We knocked on the doors of haunted-looking older men living in Portola Hill, handed them Styrofoam containers, and sometimes chatted for a moment or two. We quit Project Open Hand after a few months because Greg said he doubted he'd make it to the age of the men we served, and it was just too painful to keep doing. I gave

Greg a key to my apartment. He went out on dates every now and again but never seemed to like anyone enough to see them twice. Not at all interested in my new friends, Greg wanted to spend time with me and only me. We drank bottles of wine and took acid. Once, I swear, we shared a hallucination of a half-dozen red roses becoming one long-stemmed white rose in a vase that quivered on the bookshelf. He reminded me to take care of myself and eat bananas. And to always use condoms during sex. I sometimes ate a banana, but I almost never had a condom on hand when I needed one.

In 1993, a year into taking AZT, Greg was still a young man, in his twenties. He teetered between hopefulness that the medicine might work and shame for being a diseased, ruined person. Sometimes I found him sitting in the dark, waiting for me to get home from work.

Greg's mother, a bad drunk, had abandoned her family when Greg was a child. His father remarried a kind and motherly woman who raised Greg and his brother from elementary school through college. He adored his father and stepmother, and so did I as I got to know them, seated at their dinner table in San Jose. Traveling down to visit them on Caltrain, I saw the underbelly of The City's growing homeless population as I rolled through the south side of San Francisco. Then came the old-neighborhood charm of the blue-collar stations at San Bruno, Millbrae, and Burlingame, then the upper-middle-class suburban stops at Menlo Park, Palo Alto, and Sunnyvale, that last the station where Greg picked me up.

Those family times did wonders for both of our dispositions. Back at my studio, however, we drank and

Greg's mean streak clashed with mine. He picked on me, criticized the way I didn't make enough money and wasted my potential. He didn't approve of my multiple boyfriends, thought the country music I loved was stupid, and said I reminded him of his piece-of-shit mother. Because he was so sick, I'd try to stomach my hurt feelings, but sometimes I'd tell him to shut the fuck up and leave if he didn't want to be my friend, and then he would beg me to forgive his outbursts.

I always did. One remorseful morning he asked me to marry him. I could then inherit what was left of his cashed-out life insurance when he died. He wanted to repay me for putting up with him, plus, he wanted me to have a better future. He brought fresh-cut flowers and fancy groceries, like fresh raspberries and cream, to thank me for letting him stay at my apartment. But by that time, I could barely stand to have him there for more than a day at a time, let alone marry him. I declined his marriage offer and he left, infuriated.

Greg then flew around the world on what was left of his money and became both a party boy and an AIDS activist. I went to poetry readings and wrote songs, walked San Francisco's sidewalks full of appreciation for its culture and beauty, and worked my ass off at as many cocktailing shifts as I could get. I started dating a young, long-haired metal dude who worked as a doorman at the Improv and was sweeter than I knew metal dudes could be. His wavy hair wrapped around me like seaweed. I'd untangle myself and rise from his sheetless mattress on the floor to use the bathroom he shared with two other guys. Since there was no toilet paper, I wiped my butt on one of the stiff towels draped over a rack. Through it all, Greg and I stayed in touch. From Washington, DC, AIDS March and Ben & Jerry's rallies, Greg sent me postcards and photos. I sent letters to him at his parents' address. His illness progressed, and the calls grew further apart and then stalled out altogether.

I dug deeper into the local music scene, and my circle of friends grew big and strong while my dating life stayed chaotic. I did not ask my partners to wear condoms, although some did of their own accord by now. Not hearing from Greg worried me, and I asked, "Are you still alive?"

The day came when I received the call. Greg had returned home to die, his father told me, and hospice came daily to their house. He asked me to come down and join Greg's family and friends to say goodbye. I said I'd be there as soon as I could rent a car.

I panicked. My driver's license had expired. I ran the twelve blocks to Enterprise on Van Ness anyway, a shaking mess, hoping they wouldn't notice the date on the license. They noticed. They also watched me sob and listened to my sad story. One of the agents drove me to the DMV on Fell Street, waited in line with me to get my license renewed, then drove me back to the lot and helped me into a Ford Focus. Thanks to their kindness, I was hurtling that tin can eighty-five miles an hour down the 101 just a few hours after talking to Greg's father on the phone.

But by the time I got there, he had lost consciousness. We sat in a semicircle around him and patted his arms, covered in purple splotches from the sarcoma consuming his body. We each kissed his brow. Choked with tears, I whispered, "I love you and will miss you, Greg." Then we told stories about our beloved friend and tossed the Kleenex box back and forth over his swaddled body. We cried and cried and cried. Greg's stepmother fed us, and his dad, a man about to lose his son, took me aside and thanked me for loving his difficult child with such steadfastness. The tenderness, the strangeness of death, the rueful and silly stories we told each other about Greg, all that love and loss, we wound around each other like the sheets that held that young man's body.

At the funeral, Greg's father released twenty-eight white doves, one for each year of Greg's life.

Warmly Imagined Memory

> *I am southbound on the Caltrain*
> *headed for my boy's birthday party in San Jose*
> *My eyes hurt*
> *They are huge and achy as porcelain as a doll's*
> *good for seeing without clarity*
> *What had you looked like last night*
> *sleeping naked in your sleeping bag on your*
> *sheetless bed*
> *cluttered with old newspapers and letters and bills*
> *Birds collect string and paper and styrofoam cup*
> *pieces when they build their nests*
> *I think you are part tern*

Sandra Austin Mello

If you were here riding with me
Southbound on the Caltrain
We could lean upon each other and the window and
nap
I'd hum a lullaby—our temperatures, and
breathing conspired

Chapter 8 - Night-Blooming Cereus

After Greg's funeral, I took three days off from work and stockpiled booze, cigarettes, and cat food. Three days to wander in the wilderness. The thought crossed my mind that the loss might provide grist for my songwriting mill. I apologized to Greg for thinking that. I closed the sheets I had artfully hung in the bay window as drapes to block out any sunlight lurking behind the fog. I made coffee and ate an egg and a piece of toast. Then I poured myself a shot of bourbon and cracked open a beer. I went to the living room and pushed play on the boombox and listened to Charlie's CD. His woeful tenor dripped down the walls of my studio.

  Centered in the bay window was a brown vinyl settee with brass-tack studs adorning its seams: one of the first curb gifts San Francisco gave me after I'd moved in. I had dragged that piece of furniture home on two of its four legs. They needed serious restoration after the journey along the sidewalk, up the cement steps into my building, and across the lobby to the elevator that had filed the legs to sharp points. I'd plunked the thing down in the middle of my living room on a paint-flecked bedsheet I kept folded with my art supplies and scrubbed the settee clean, then rubbed the vinyl to a warm luster with shoe polish. I painted the mangled legs bronze.

Now, in my dim living room where Greg would never drink wine with me again, I made the settee into an altar. I lined up the supplies I needed to grieve properly: a full quart of Jim Beam, an empty glass, my boombox, an ashtray, a Bic lighter, and a box of Marlboro Reds. I lit a candle and pushed play.

I sat in a forest of tenor notes and cried more for myself than for Greg. My loss, my struggles, my ransacked heart. After I drained the bourbon I filled the claw-foot tub and took a hot bath. I woke up wrinkled in cold water and felt nauseous. I got dressed, went to the corner store to re-up supplies, kept my sunglasses on inside the store, bought more cigarettes than I thought I'd need, and got back to the apartment just as the sun went down. I played Charlie's CD some more, fell asleep, woke up, masturbated, fell back asleep, woke up, wrote for hours, and emptied a twelve-pack of Schaefer beer. I took the elevator to the rooftop sometime in the middle of the night and whimpered—feeble, confused, and angry. I pleaded with the universe to show me the way. I knew I drank too much. Had I not been a good enough friend to Greg? Since I felt guilty, suffering seemed like the right penance. Then I wobbled back down to my apartment, slept for a while, and continued to do what I knew best: write about the anguish with the soft sweater of alcohol wrapped around me so I did not have to feel so cold and left behind.

I suffered for as long as I could stand it, then music saved me once again. It drew me out of my bender and out to a live show. I needed music and other people because I was sick to death of Charlie's music and mourning Greg.

Hell-bent on learning as much as I could about country music, I became a barnacle at every record store within walking distance. Being country-fluent would ingratiate me into the world of Charlie. I still held out hope that our time would come and we could be together as a real couple. In the meantime, I might meet someone who could make me happy. After work and on my days off I recorded original songs and sang them a cappella onto cassettes, then slipped the fledgling newborns in between recordings by Lucinda Williams, Jann Browne, Emmylou Harris, and Neil Young on my mixtapes. By absorbing country music's essence, I hoped to wring it out into my songs. I gave these cassettes to Billy and mailed copies to Linden in Prague and my friends in Southern California.

Once, while cleaning the headliner's condo on Nob Hill, the vacuum cleaner broke. Something too big got sucked up, stuck, and burned up a belt. The smell of scorched rubber reminded me of how my mother made pudding. She wouldn't stir it enough as it thickened on the stovetop, then would claim the burned bottom made it taste like butterscotch even though it started out as vanilla. I stashed the broken machine in a closet and instead of asking for new equipment, I used strips of masking tape wrapped around my hand to pick up obvious pieces of crap off the carpet. The experience of killing a vacuum cleaner begat a song. Like a spit bubble, the melody and words emerged, a fully formed country-blues melody à la The

Blasters. I heard slide guitar. It was dark and menacing, a story with uneven edges.

Small Messes

There was a murder at the hotel / evidence left by the side

I was cleaning small messes when the smoke began to rise

Smoke strangled the last breath / a monster's final writhe

Exhale by the bereft / relief I can't deny

A murder has been committed / Even though nobody died

I've been made an accomplice / My crime to run and hide

The hunt for a band began in earnest. I had been here for nine months, and I needed something to show for it. Competitive, I didn't intend to stay a second-place girlfriend forever. I wanted to knock everyone who thought they knew me on their asses.

I clomped down Haight Street, skirting packs of runaway kids and their dogs spread out on the sidewalk, dropping change into the rusty Alpo cans, hoping they'd spend it on dog food. I passed the Haight Ashbury Free Clinic, where I would be prescribed penicillin later that winter when my cough turned phlegmy, ripped through my chest, and left a strangely sweet taste in my mouth. Bronchitis wouldn't stop me from smoking on the sidewalk outside the clinic, slouched in my thick Persian wool coat, waiting for my prescription. I nodded at the post office where I mailed my mixtapes. I stared up at the I-Beam nightclub as I walked under the marquee and thought about dancing there with Greg until we were sweaty and senseless. Then I opened the door and tucked into the aisles of Haight Ashbury Music Center, hoping to rub shoulders with one of the local musicians I admired.

  A sign on the musicians' bulletin board read "George looking for Tammy." A classic country reference I sort of understood. And, hosanna, a band that looked good! I had not sung in a band in over a decade, not since 1982, and that had been ill-fated—a short run with a Top 40 cover band from central Florida called Alpha Six. Alpha Six toured Ramada Inns along the Atlantic seaboard and I sang the lead on Donna Summer, Juice Newton, and Sheena Easton songs. (I'd auditioned with an a cappella version of Pat Benatar's "Hell Is for Children.") That band broke up five shows into its first tour, and I caught a Greyhound bus back to Orlando.

  Rusty or not, I set up a time to meet with "George" and went for it as "Tammy." In the week preceding, I practiced Ms. Wynette's delivery and tried to sound as much like the original Steel Magnolia as I could. And what do you know, the first band I auditioned for in San Francisco asked me to join them that very day. I became the newest member of Western Electric as the winsome sidekick on duets and harmonies. I learned the band's material from a rehearsal tape featuring the former Tammy, who happened to be none other than "Wholesome" Jill Olson from the aforementioned Red Meat and the Movie Stars.

Western Electric rehearsed once a week in Novato, a small town in Marin County, which was difficult to get to since I did not have a car. A friend told me about a bus route that went over the bridge. To get to the closest stop, I'd leave my studio in the Western Addition, walk up Fulton, wave at Alamo Square, turn right at Eddie's Cafe, where I ordered eggs and raisin toast when I met friends for breakfast, and then hoof it up and down the hills of Divisadero to Lombard Street. Once there, I'd wait for the bus, which, after it got over the Golden Gate, seemed to meander rather than drive through Marin City, Sausalito, and my stop, Novato. It took two to three hours in each direction for an hour-long band rehearsal, yet every minute of the trek felt worth it. I lunged at the opportunity.

Being in Western Electric made me feel legit. I now sang in an established band with real gigs. Cary Hansen played guitar, sang lead, and wrote the songs. Sir Spooky played bass and sang harmonies. The drummer, Robert, was a former member of the roots-rockabilly band The Paladins, from San Diego, and a rotating cast of pedal steel players swirled in and out. Blackie Farrell played with us on occasion, or just hung out and drank beers during practice since he and Cary were buddies.

The rehearsals filled me up. I loved to sing, and it felt good to meet musicians. We practiced in Cary's living room on a wooded street in Novato where Grace Slick was rumored to live a block away. The guys were great musicians and serious gossipers. They told scandalous stories about musicians they had worked with, and I regaled them with stories about famous comedians and, of course, Charlie, whose music they admired. Sometimes we barbecued on the patio afterward, and sometimes I got a ride back to SF with Sir Spooky or, with increasing frequency, the rockabilly drummer, Robert.

But when I didn't get a ride and took the bus home instead, my insides hollowed out like a rotted tree stump. I climbed aboard the air-conditioned vehicle and chose a seat at a westward-facing window. These buses that ran between the city and the suburbs were so much nicer and better maintained than the city bus lines. Yet all that effort to get to and from rehearsal caught up with me as I settled myself, emotional and drained. The cushioned seat cradling me and the gentle rocking motion of the bus as it lumbered up the Sausalito hills made me think about my mom. I felt bad for her and I missed her. Life had been hard for my mom, and I did nothing to make it better.

The year before I moved to San Francisco, my single mother had moved to Southern California with my youngest brother in tow. She said she wanted to be nearer to me, and I stood tall with the hope to help. Because she did not drive, I drove her to and from work at Bullock's in South Coast Plaza in Costa Mesa, and to the grocery store on her days off. My little brother could ride his bike to school but, still, the logistics of juggling two households' driving schedules became more than I could handle. When the Improv sent us to San Francisco for three months, Mom decided she and my little brother would move back to Orlando. I felt guilty about all of it. I had encouraged them to come to California, then abandoned them. These days I could barely support myself, let alone help her. I knew Mom was disappointed in me.

I scanned the backs of the other passengers' heads and landed on an arbitrary middle-aged woman with wavy brown hair. *That's her! Mom's taken the bus all the way across the country to surprise me.* I played this wretched game long enough to feel good and sorry for myself. I wrote a note on the back of a sheet of song lyrics—"hereditary headache"—then chronicled my fucked DNA: Mom's depression and migraines and Dad's schizophrenia. I jostled in my seat, forlorn and raw, as I gazed at the white sailboats in the blue harbor, then the breathtaking rise of the Golden Gate Bridge over the Pacific. It all blurred with tears.

Performing in a band boosted my fragile self-esteem. Now I had something to write home about: proof that I could succeed as an artist. I sent pictures of myself on stage to my mother and siblings and friends in SoCal. I met more and more musicians at shows and rehearsals. I did not spend much of my hard-earned tips on new clothes, but stage wear became the exception. I found a blue velvet skirt with white polka dots on sale at the Betsey Johnson shop on Fillmore. I wore that skirt on stage with a vintage men's suit vest, a black-beaded rosary around my neck, and oxblood lace-up pointed-toe Doc Martens boots. We played the Bottom of the Hill, the Ace Café, the various stages of the Paradise Lounge, and backyard barbecues.

I felt anxious and scared for the first song or two of each set, before my hearing adjusted to the loud amps and PA. Once I got used to the stage sound, I loved being part of something bigger than me, letting loose my energy into the big mix. I closed my eyes when I sang the scary parts, the ones where I got to belt. Like sex, singing overtook my body and mind. My lips grazed the microphone and my voice burst from the speakers. I sizzled while being watched. I tried to be careful about how much I drank before we went on, swigging just enough to release the genie but not give away all my wishes. Like, not sucking. Afterward, I drank to win. I needed go-go juice to carry me through the rest of the night and its long, analytical conversations: how we compared to the other bands, the turnout, the pay, the next gig, and of course the hoped-for compliments.

Dear Sound Person,
Thank you for the reverb.

By now, I knew my way around San Francisco and had acquired a habit of roaming the near-empty sidewalks late at night, most often by myself and sometimes in a blackout. After a gig, after work, after leaving a bar, I'd find myself walking, even striding along, completely unaware of where I was or how I'd got there. A flesh package with no address, my body did not need me to tell it where to go; it just went. The lure of the moon pulled me open like a night-blooming cereus. I came to in various parts of The City at quiet hours: leaning over the railing of the Stockton Street tunnel above Chinatown just before dawn and rush hour; at the crest of the hill on Fillmore Street listening to foghorns; on Ellis Street in the Tenderloin outside of Jonell's Cocktail Lounge while the bar back washed down the sidewalk with a hose. I came to while eating falafel in front of Truly Mediterranean on 16th Street, as conscious as a leaf on the breeze with tzatziki sauce dripping down my chin. Hoofing along late at night, I sang the country songs I learned for my band. Sometimes loud enough to have someone yell from a window above to quiet the fuck down. I sang in self-defense. No one wanted to mess with a weirdo singing "Sparkling Brown Eyes" at two in the morning.

There's a rambled shackle shack down in North Caroliney...

When the dangerous behavior of the night before poked through the gaggy veil of a hangover, I withered. Fear morphed into awe. I wondered if the supernatural worked through me. It seemed beyond lucky that I had gotten away with being out on the streets in a blackout—again. I became a giddy ghost rider of my own life. Fear of my lack of control simmered in my gut, and I told myself I was a blessed loose cannon.

Some nights I hauled a coffee can full of coins to the corner market at, say, a quarter to two, just in time to get a quart of Colt 45 and a pack of smokes before they stopped selling liquor at 2 am. My goal: pass out before I run out. Since I required more and more alcohol to knock me out, I rotated which stores I went to for the sake of appearances. The men who ran those stores knew me; I had been a customer for almost a year now. We were friendly during the day and even on a first-name basis when I popped in for a pack of smokes or some milk, but on these other shopping runs they looked at me with such pity, I had to widen the radius of corner stores so I could count out pennies, nickels, and dimes to an unconcerned cashier.

One night I came to a block from my apartment. My almost-vintage Guess watch said it was after two, which meant the corner store with *Ebony* magazine at the counter and cheap forties was closed. But I was out of cigarettes. The only other person still out on the street besides me was a homeless man pushing a Safeway cart full of old blankets and empty plastic soda bottles. I asked if he had a spare cigarette. He said yes and that I could have it for a kiss. He held the cigarette out to me and opened his wet red mouth. My soul split town but I got a cigarette, and that's what mattered. When that memory greeted my waking thoughts, I decided not to tell anyone about it.

Several months into singing with Western Electric, we opened for the rootsy-rock songwriter Mark Curry at Slim's. I'd seen dozens of major acts at this well-known venue, including Charlie, and it was a big deal to play there. I drank to quell my nerves before we went on. If I could keep it together before showtime I would get my reward afterward. On this night, I missed the mark.

A smattering of well-dressed African American couples stood in front of the stage. We dug into a few country duets, Tammy and George's "We're Not the Jet Set" followed by a rootsy country rocker by Carlene Carter and Dave Edmunds, "Baby Ride Easy." One pair after another of well-dressed couples left the stage area and clustered at the door to get their money back. Turns out, they thought Mark Curry the headliner was Mark Curry the comedian. By the time we closed out our set with the Gram Parsons and Emmylou Harris duet "Ooh, Las Vegas," a few of my friends and a handful of stragglers remained to witness my wasted glory. Billy and Mia smiled at me. I smiled back and tried to hit the super-high notes, but it took more effort than I could muster, and my vocal skidded off somewhere to the side of the stage, nowhere near the harmony with Cary. I don't remember Mark Curry's set. I had embarrassed myself and felt like I'd blown the band's chances for more gigs at Slim's. My friends assured me it wasn't that bad, but I knew they were just being nice. I couldn't look my bandmates in the eye, other than the drummer, who would not care about my disgrace since I was pretty sure the possibility of sex with me was more important to him than my singing abilities. There was so much to worry about.

By this time, I had had enough of working at the Warfield. The bulk of my friends had already quit, and sometimes I didn't make enough in tips to cover the cost of transportation to and from a night shift. When Pantera played to a house full of bridge-and-tunnel juvenile boys, indignant at what a Coke cost in a showroom and with no experience tipping, it dawned on me how shitty my job was. I spent most of that earsplitting show cowering in the empty upstairs women's bathroom. That same week, as I walked to work, I came across a dead body on the sidewalk just a few blocks from the Warfield. At least, I assumed he was dead, since bloody-looking stuff was pooled under his head. I did not know what to do but walk faster and get away from the horror. My next scheduled shift was an Allman Brothers show—a prospect so unappealing, I called my supervisor and quit over the phone. I couldn't brave another walk to work for a band I didn't care about.

As I strode up and down San Francisco's steep hills and dirty sidewalks, I realized I had changed, that I was a different woman than the one who'd arrived from Orange County. I was less buoyant and bright-eyed, more realistic and world-wearier. I was becoming a tough old broad. I had lived on my own for nine months, and even though there was plenty of charm all around me, there wasn't enough money. I had been scrappy and would continue to find my way. But it was time to look for someplace more affordable to live. I had burned through my nest egg, and the Warfield revenue was gone. The roots I had grown in the El Bethel neighborhood would have to be pulled up. If I didn't deposit my tips right away, I spent them, and even if I did make it to the bank, my account still emptied out between paltry paychecks. Top Ramen, Mission burritos, and eggs fed me. I bought my clothes from penny-a-pound. I borrowed books, bought cutout CDs, and went to cheaper matinees. I didn't have a car, insurance of any kind, a television, cable, or a heating bill. Rent, alcohol and cigarettes, cat food and litter, bus fare, live music, and the occasional cab bled me dry. How steep the mountain my $525 monthly rent had become!

I scrambled to get another waitstaff job and found one nearby at the Good Earth Café in Japantown. The cinnamon tea and fresh-baked-bran-muffin-smelling environment wrapped me in its wholesome arms. But soon after, Charlie came through town. The phone rang and his voice said the magic words, "I miss you. Ride with me to LA?"

"How soon will you be here?" I said.

"About an hour," he replied.

"See you soon."

I showered and fixed my hair, put on a clean pair of jeans and my coolest 1960s striped knit top, and tossed my makeup and a change of clothes into an overnight bag. I filled Nellie's bowls to the brim, scruffed her cheeks, and kissed her on the top of the head before running down the three flights of stairs to wait at the curb. Charlie pulled up, and I hopped into his rental car. We looked at each other and burst into laughter.

Instead of showing up for work, I kept Charlie company down the hypnotic I-5 freeway to Los Angeles. We ate chicken sandwiches on soft white bread made by the wife of the owner of the venue in Davis where he'd gigged the night before. I didn't even bother calling in with an excuse for missing my shift, nor did I pick up my last paycheck. While I was in LA, my ex-husband and I had lunch and compared notes about our bitchin' new love lives. Because I was covered in bruises from rough sex and sharp corners and had not slept in forty-eight hours, he assumed I now shot heroin. I assured Brad that needles scared me too much and joked that I'd shoot heroin in the old folks' home when I had nothing left to lose.

Swollen Appetite

The Good Earth revenue ended, but my relationship with Charlie was back on. Wild breath filled my sails as I floated back into San Francisco on the tail end of the reckless trip to LA and into my next shift at the Improv. How I loved that crew and their appetite to hear my stories. My coworkers suggested I look for roommates if I couldn't make ends meet; that was how they were able to afford The City. The rental agency allowed me to end my lease a few months early, and so, with much sadness, I left the first nest I'd built in San Francisco. I said goodbye to my view of the elaborate Victorian Chateau Tivoli across the street, the white-paint outline of the suicide body on the sidewalk below, and the neighborhood where I'd learned more about Southern Black culture than in my entire youth growing up in the South.

Chapter 9 - Laid a Golden Egg

On the corner of Broderick and McAllister, I rented a room in an apartment with two white professional men fresh out of college. Through their younger eyes, I saw myself: an older woman in a band who worked at a comedy club and sometimes dated a semi-famous singer. I was salty and cool. The soles of my boots had worn down and my leather jacket had been broken in. These guys distracted me from how bad it felt to be unable to afford my own studio.

New to living with strangers, I wanted my roommates to like me. I spun stories from illustrious days of yore—that time I sat on the patio of the Irvine Improv and helped Rosie O'Donnell make a Halloween costume: we sewed toy cars in a jig-jagged way along the white stripe of her black sweatpants to represent traffic on the 405. How I rode in a vintage hearse-limo with Johnny Thunders when he toured San Diego. What it had been like to watch The Pixies and Jane's Addiction when they first started out and played shows at smallish clubs in Southern California. My easy-to-impress roomies learned about the New York Dolls and slurped up my stories over the community pots of potato soup, chicken chili, and Bolognese with pasta that I gladly cooked for us.

The flat we shared was unexceptional. No glass doorknobs, fancy moldings, or built-in bookshelves. Two bedrooms sat on opposite ends, and the living room had been converted into a bedroom; the sliding doors that separated it from the dining room allowed privacy. The three of us shared one bathroom. Good at opening drawers, Nellie burrowed in the bottom drawer of one of my new roommates' dressers and napped in between his socks and T-shirts. Good thing for us he liked cats.

The common spaces of the apartment were messy. For a wild woman, I had high cleanliness standards. I scrubbed the tub, toilet, and kitchen sink. I tried to make the bland apartment more attractive by hanging art in the hallways and filling flowerpots on the back porch with marigolds and ferns. I crammed as many of my belongings as would fit into my bedroom and the dining room; the rest I sold or gave away. My bedroom perched above the street sign on the corner, and the east-facing pop-out window stayed open no matter the weather because the bedroom seemed the only polite place inside the apartment to smoke.

On an antique table in front of my bedroom window, I placed a croton plant from my granddaddy's nursery in Florida. That plant had traveled across the country in the back of my boyfriend's VW Scirocco, along with our cat and everything we owned, ten years earlier when I left Orange County, Florida, for Orange County, California. It had grown bushy and beautiful. I watered the rich potting soil beneath the glossy green leaves veined with vermillion while I looked out the window and watched drugs being sold behind the corner store. That worried me a little. Even though I drank gallons of booze a week, I only did drugs if someone gave them to me. Burned pieces of aluminum, dismantled pen parts, and used condoms littered the sidewalks and gutters on my three-block walk to Haight Street. This neighborhood, unlike the Western Addition, lacked a specific style or character. I couldn't get a handle on who lived in these uninteresting apartment buildings. My previous neighborhood had Victorians, Baptist churches, parks, and a community feel. Still, I liked my new roommates. Living with others made me a little more thoughtful, and kept despair at bay. I sang! I gigged! I wrote new poetry and more songs. My roommates brought their friends to my shows.

Charlie called in a surly mood. I had not heard from him in at least six weeks, not since our LA trip. I hated waiting around for him to call but did not want to appear too eager or needy by calling him first. Concerned by his tone of voice, I asked what was so troubling.

"My record label dropped me," he said. He might have been drunk.

"Wow, that sucks. What stupid assholes! Is there anything I could do to make you feel better?" I expected a little phone sex.

"You could loan me fifty thousand dollars for my next release," he slurred.

I gasped. Charlie backpedaled and tried to play it off as a joke. It did not take us long to hang up on each other. I worried for a few minutes that I had done something wrong. A few drinks later, my shaky ship crested on a sea of anger. *He* was supposed to help *me*, goddammit, not the other way around!

I began to spend more and more time with Robert, the drummer from Western Electric, at his large apartment off Taraval. We had the band and our stints in San Diego in common. When Candye Kane, a San Diego blues artist, came through Northern California, he played drums in her band. I saw Reno for the first time on a short tour as one of Candye's crew, and she had me lace up her corset—a true feat to wrangle her legendary bosom—while we got loaded before a small, shitty casino gig. Downright raunchy in her persona, Candye was also a crazy-good blues singer. She kept pushing me to sing with her but I was too intimidated, too insecure to even try. On the drive home to San Francisco, she introduced me to the music of a new singer-songwriter, Iris Dement. I fell in love with Iris's church-lady voice as it flew through the tops of the Ponderosa pine trees along the hilly roadside.

Living with roommates wasn't as bad as I thought it would be. They were nice guys; they fed Nellie when I spent the night out at Robert's apartment. Robert and I did not fall in love or get too hung up on knowing each other well. We palled around. Western Electric gigged plenty, and those several shows a month, along with hanging out and listening to music, watching TV, and sleeping together, was enough to sustain us. I had plenty of shifts at the Improv. The days had a nice hum and an engaging rhythm. Then one night the phone rang and woke me from the disco nap I was taking before meeting Billy and Mia in the Lower Haight at eleven. Napping was my new strategy to drink less—it helped me prolong the time before I got started.

On the phone, the voice of a man I had fallen in love with right after graduating from high school in Tennessee said he had me on his mind. He was calling from Switzerland, where he was working the Montreux Jazz Festival on Emmylou Harris's summer tour. After just a few minutes of catch-up, he said he was sad and lonely. I said I was sad and lonely, too. We coiled around each other, a swirl of chemistry that traveled over miles and miles of phone cable stretching across the ocean floor and several time zones. We spoke about the last time we'd seen each other and our failed marriages and made a plan to meet once again in Nashville. I did not worry too much about how that would affect things with the drummer.

Stacks of journals I had filled in my first San Francisco studio apartment brimmed with lists of what I did and did not want, and used all of the college words I could spell. No crevice escaped my lingering gaze, and I wrote with a candor I had not known. Sophisticated and depraved, full of bravado, I played with words and the desire to be ripped apart. I needed to self-destruct and to wriggle through the jagged rocks and broken pieces of bone that lined the crawlspace to my psyche. I had turned into a warrior of sorts, shooting arrows into the dark and pinning pain to the page.

Victor, the Tennessee boyfriend who had called me up from halfway around the world, had not yet made his way into my drunken journals, my artist's ledger of pages splotched with tears, wine, melted wax, cigarette ash, and doodles alongside heavily underlined and circled words. I reveled in the abrasion of my skin during rough sex, and the calluses and blisters from hours of walking in heavy boots. With self-cruelty, I poked at the bruises and scrapes I found on my body in the shower after a night of blacking out. The sensations fascinated me. I felt proud of all the emotional ups and downs I could now withstand, especially what I felt after losing Greg and breaking up with Charlie. Even my first bourgeois marriage that I'd pretended didn't matter had gutted me. Because of all of that, I was stronger and wiser.

Victor and I had had a rough-and-tumble history, and the light inside me dimmed as I shuddered in excitement. More ouchy-wow-wow was headed my way. Could I wrangle him now that I was no longer a timid, unmoored teenager, but rather a tough city woman? The relationship with him post–high school had left me shaky. A few years older than me, he had seemed so adult and together, mysterious even, and I had waded knee-deep into the murk of what he didn't say. I tried to act cooler than I was by taking too many drugs, drugs he always had on hand. The summer after I graduated, a group of us formed a band and lived in Victor's apartment outside of Nashville. While he worked a real job during the day, we unemployed bandmates slouched on the threadbare couch and watched *General Hospital* and MTV, smoked cigarettes, and got high. I had zero dollars. We shared everything, from cigarettes to beer. I shoplifted a box of blueberry muffin mix from a nearby grocery store and made them for us to eat while we celebrated the day Luke and Laura got married on *GH*. Somebody in the band had a handful of Valium.

But not knowing if Victor loved me back made me feel icky enough to call my older brother, who sent me a hundred dollars for gas money to Florida; I fled and stayed with him until I got myself together.

That was then; now our sodden hearts hung on each end of that long-distance phone call from Europe. He worked for Emmylou Harris and had said that he needed me.

Victor's scene, and the people I had partied with in Nashville, hid their bad behavior. Naughty under their button-down collars, pockets filled with Visine, Certs, and Quaaludes, they liked to sneak around and keep secrets. I had grown to love flaunting my wild side in San Francisco. Being brazen excited me, but brazen would not fly in Tennessee, so I would have to tamp that shit down. My siblings lived near Nashville, so it made perfect sense for me to fly out, visit my family, and have a fling with a man who had deflated me in the past even though he wore pressed jeans and hair spray.

Downright giddy with sexual power, I waited to be picked up at the airport. The short baby-doll dress I wore had been discovered at a new used-clothing store on Fillmore Street named Crossroads. Black knee socks rose out of my pointy-toe Docs, exposing several inches of pale bare thigh. My guy found me, said, "nice legs," and rushed me along to his car. We had to hurry to a photo shoot: his boss, Emmylou Harris, was being photographed for the album cover of *Cowgirl's Prayer*. In the airport parking lot, we lingered just long enough to get high and kiss before speeding over to the east side of town.

This was my first big celebrity photo shoot. I had been to TV-show tapings with my ex in Southern California and had shared the back seat of a small Honda with Adam Sandler and David Spade all the way from Irvine to Burbank, where Adam was performing his first stand-up appearance on *The Tonight Show* with Johnny Carson. But to behold a superstar musician I revered having her picture taken over and over again reached new heights of coolness. Professional lighting had been set up inside an old, dilapidated warehouse with busted-out windows, crumbling red brick, and thick flowering vines creeping in from the outside. Broken glass and rubble littered the cracked cement floor, adding to the mood, and the goddess herself posed less than ten yards from where we stood. Emmylou's long legs dangled over the edge of a staircase and disappeared into a pair of inlaid white cowboy boots. With a steady gaze, the most elegant of cowgirls peered into the cameras and said, "The legs are the last thing to go."

Victor took me back to his house in the suburbs. He asked me to lie low during business hours the next day because he had an assistant who worked part-time in the home office. I wondered why it mattered but went along with it, pacing back and forth in the master bedroom like a caged tiger. I watched hours of MTV and CMT, and did sit-ups and leg lifts. Blew cigarette smoke out a cracked window. Took a long shower. But when I couldn't stand it any longer, I snuck down the stairs to the kitchen for a snack.

The assistant must have seen me. Victor later explained that they'd had a brief affair but had decided not to mix business with pleasure. He wanted to be considerate of her feelings by not parading me in front of her. I didn't believe him for a second. Maybe that affair wasn't finished, or maybe Victor didn't want word to get back to the wife he had not yet divorced, with whom he shared custody of a child he adored. I bristled but kept my doubts to myself. I kept hoping the way I felt about him and the way he felt about me would become clearer.

I flew home and resumed my San Francisco life. Victor and I continued to see each other as Emmylou's touring schedule ramped up and she played California more often. I started to think that maybe we had a future together. Sure, he treated me like a mistress, but that could change.

Singing in Western Electric, waiting tables for a living, and sharing a small apartment with two roommates in a shitty neighborhood looked shabby as I orbited Emmylou's organization: a well-oiled machine with great talent, big crews, big venues, and nice hotels. I had stumbled into a fairy tale and hoped to lay a golden egg of my own. Tumbling back and forth between the world of an established musician and my own made my artistic achievements seem puny. I felt stuck in a too-small shell and knocked loose at the same time. I knew I could do what Emmylou did with enough help. I would spend two or three days in a row with Victor and the tour—however many work shifts I could get covered—then the tour would travel to a different part of the country and I'd return to my neglected life. Then they'd roar through the Bay Area again.

    I rode with Victor in the front of the tour bus as it cruised down the I-5 corridor from San Francisco to LA and got to know the members of the band. Although Emmylou did not participate in the after-show parties or get stoned on the bus with us, we spoke every now and then. She lamented a milkshake she'd had earlier in the day, so now she couldn't have a peach. I did not understand why she couldn't have both. She said I'd find out as I grew older and my metabolism slowed down. But mostly, she kept to herself in her suite in the back of the bus.

    On a plane at LAX, I slunk down in my window seat and waited for takeoff. I found a piece of opium the size of a pinkie nail in the pocket of my jeans I'd worn the night before when Emmylou performed at the Wiltern in Los Angeles. I chewed the tarry nugget of opium, and it reminded me of the Dutch licorice a friend used to bring home from Amsterdam. Tonight, Emmylou would play a private house concert in Orinda. As the opium kicked in, spatial misconceptions flooded me. I could not tell where my body ended and the plane began. An important storyline emerged as I thought I could see through the plastic cabin molding to the welded metal casing of the outside of the plane. My life force oozed into the alloy and rivets that held the plane together—that fodder in the chinks was me—and if I didn't pay attention, we'd blow apart twenty thousand feet above the Earth. We had not yet left the gate and people were still boarding the plane. A friend from the tour peeled me away from the wall and put a Valium in my palm. I chewed it like I had chewed the opium. The row behind us remained empty until minutes before takeoff. At the last possible moment, a priest, a woman tanned to the color of chewing tobacco, and her spiky-white-haired companion boarded and took the seats behind us. White-hair guy bitched out loud as he squished down the aisle. Turns out the whiner was none other than John Lydon, aka Johnny Rotten. That's when I knew the plane would crash and I did not have the strength to hold it together.

    A short while later, the Valium kicked in and I fell asleep.

The party ended when Victor went back to Nashville without asking me to move in with him. The drummer from Western Electric and I called it quits but remained friends. I returned to my boring life waiting tables at the Improv. Sans the celebrities, life's effervescence fizzled. I twisted in bitterness and begrudged my exes who were all doing so well with their lives while nothing noteworthy took place in mine. Super late and super drunk, I called Victor. I asked him to marry me as soon as his divorce was final.

    He said no. He said it nicely.

    In my small bedroom, anger motivated my output, as did the comics' performances I scrutinized at the Improv. I doubled down on my writing efforts.

Multitalented

Separate baby
Put the whites in one bowl and the yolks in another

Swollen Appetite

They warn us with yellows
But   FUCK   EGGS
They have only two cells
You are holding twelve baskets
sleeping alone but wanting a master
You are haunted but funny
Cracking up strangers
Eating her ovaries
not sure if you can make it to the next gig

Chapter 10 - Three Decades of Me

I began to appreciate San Francisco again. How could I not? Perched over the Pacific Ocean, she overflowed with beauty and culture and magnificent people. My talented and intriguing friends revived me. I was still close to French kickboxer Chloe and Jolisa from the Warfield, as well as Mia and Billy from the Improv. Then I became close with one of the Improv's bookkeepers. My new friend, Fiona, was younger than me, yet had perfected cynicism by her early twenties. Pale and sophisticated, with long fingernails like Barbara Streisand and thick hair that fell in cold currents past her bra strap, she possessed a Gothic chill even when dressed in canary yellow. A dark-haired Sylvia Plath, Fiona had a degree in comparative lit from San Francisco State and wore an eyebrow ring before anyone else I knew. She referenced authors with authority and pointed out the holes in other people's reasoning. Fiona had written poetry in college, and like Linden, she didn't let me read it.

Her educated circle of friends welcomed me to their parties and, after a drink or two, I'd find Fiona giggling in a corner waiting for someone to sit on the whoopee cushion she'd hidden among the couch pillows. Full of contradictions, she could knock anyone off their high horse. When ready to leave those parties, I'd find my fascinating new buddy sound asleep on top of a pile of coats on the designated coats bed, a true lightweight drinker. Almost every time we went into a public bathroom, from the anonymity of a stall, Fiona would make repulsive, wet-sounding fart noises with her hands, then exclaim, "Sandra!"

If the line was too long for breakfast at Kate's Kitchen in the Lower Haight, we'd walk a block and a half up to the Horseshoe coffee house, grab a paper and a table, and figure out men. We exchanged exasperated stories about the banal crap some comics complained about or expected: the pay, a different time slot. *Fucking prima donnas!* We read music and literary reviews over cheddar and green onion biscuits with mushroom gravy and a thousand cups of coffee.

Fiona's passion for live music matched mine. We attended show after show, going to the Bottom of Hill and the South of Market triangle of venues—Slim's, the Paradise Lounge, and the Atlas Café—the most often. Indie rock and Americana music lovers, we did not miss a show from the Bottle Rockets, The Jayhawks, the Sunshine Club, Chris Von Sneidern, or Uncle Tupelo. Once, while getting some fresh air outside the Paradise Lounge after a kick-ass set from Lucinda Williams and Gurf Morlix on the lounge stage, we saw comedian Mike Myers, in the midst of filming *So I Married an Axe Murderer*. Under our boot heels we ground out our cigarettes and declared the local poetry scene officially mainstream. Which meant I felt free to dismiss rather than refine my craft. I had switched gears for the most part anyway, pouring my passion into songwriting.

One night after my shift at the Improv, Chloe joined me at the Blue Lamp, a nearby bar on Geary Street. Its tattered majesty—faded flocked crimson and foil wallpaper, gilded mirrors, and rotted velvet batting hanging like Spanish moss in the eaves—transported me back to San Francisco's gaudy past. We smoked one cigarette after another, filling up the ashtray on the small wobbly table. Cigarette smoke, fetid wine, and decades-old spilled beer permeated every carpet fiber. The band that played that night, a rockabilly trio named The Jackdaws, seemed straight out of a David Lynch film. They reminded me of the LA trio The Havalinas, except they were less rock and more billy, more musical and less tattoo-love-boy. The lead singer and guitarist, Brian Mello, sang with the beauty and angst of John Doe and the earnestness of Johnny Cash. Entranced, I watched the reflection of my slender arm in the wall mirror as cigarette smoke snaked around it, the music making every move cinematic.

I spent my thirtieth birthday in bed, officially old, barricaded with the cat.

Late that afternoon the phone rang and rang. I pulled my pillow over my head. Later I got up and listened to voices on my answering machine: Fiona, Jolisa, Billy, and Mia all told me to get my sad-sack ass over to our beloved Puerto Alegre because they were going to treat me to a shredded beef taco and as many beers as I could drink.

Swollen Appetite

Time to celebrate being a crummy old broad. I fluffed up my curls, blotted my matte red lipstick, added several long necklaces over my thermal, and ran across Market to Church, took a left at 16th Street, where it always smelled of natural gas, and turned right on Valencia.

Beer number one paved the way. The margarita after that lightened my grip and let me laugh at myself. The countless other drinks at Doc's Clock and Dalva painted my world-weary view rosy. My mood changed—I had lived here for a scant year, for chrissakes. I plunked quarter after quarter into the extensive jukebox at Dalva. And even though fame and fortune eluded me, my friends, the night life, stacks of poems, and a growing number of original songs sustained me. There were a few gigs left with Western Electric before we took a hiatus. I had good hair and a small waist. Somewhere in this tide of musicians, true love awaited me. At thirty, it seemed too late to start over, so I just kept pounding away.

A few months later, as the Earth tilted and autumn descended, San Francisco let her fog shroud drop. Scattered like mica in granite, patches of sunlight shimmered on the pavement between the Kaiser hospital building and the parking structure across the street. The elegant fan-shaped leaves of the ginkgo trees had turned bright yellow and sifted to the sidewalk. I sat down on a greasy couch someone had discarded at the curb on Divisadero near Geary. Still inebriated, I hadn't been home since the day before. When I first moved to town, it was a triumph to not waste the night by sleeping, like I had gotten away with something. Now I wasn't so sure. Fear gripped my gut at the end of every drinking episode—that is, if I was still awake when the booze left my brain. A dreaded physical and emotional collapse was sure to follow.

Even so, the morning sun warmed me. I lit a cigarette with a shaky hand and remembered some of the night before. First I had gone to the Hotel Utah to see the Old Joe Clarks and told the lead singer, Mike, that if he ever needed more harmonies, I could sing with him. He thanked me, and without prompting, I told him I sang like Emmylou Harris. He laughed and said, "Is that right?" I felt dismissed. After that exchange, I got into a fight with the guy who took me to the show. Now I sat on the throwaway couch with no idea of the details of what happened after that fight or how I came to be sitting here, anxious with nowhere to go.

I exhaled the night from my lungs and squinted at the new day. Nothing stirred but the pigeons cooing overhead on the windowsills of apartment buildings. The morning breeze picked up, and I could feel the change in season. Defeated, I trudged home for a much-needed nap and thought about the Improv's decision to close. Which meant I would have to look for a new job. Two jobs, since my condo-cleaning gig would also end. I had worked there for nearly a year and assumed we, the waitstaff, had drunk it into the ground but didn't dare ask. And there was just one more show scheduled with Western Electric before it went on hiatus, at the Bottom of the Hill the first weekend in November.

Swollen Appetite

Pigeon Roost

I learned something just now:
where the pigeons go
They line low roofs silhouetted against
a crack of cream
The sun came up
Made me ready to
break
spill
warp the wood
The wear and tear of the pigeon roost
can't hold this weight much longer

Chapter 11 - Why Nashville?

Emmylou Harris was headed west again and Victor called to let me know when they'd land in San Francisco. Did I want to hang out? Of course, I said, and swallowed my pride even though he had declined my marriage proposal.

What perfect timing! I invited Victor to see my band's last show at the Bottom of the Hill, but sadly, it didn't work for his schedule. But just to be near Emmylou again and see her live shows with the Nash Ramblers was good enough. Those shows infused me with renewed respect for country music, in particular traditional country music, which led to the idea that Nashville might be a better destination for this budding songwriter than San Francisco. I might as well look for a new job and a new band in a new town. I mentioned this to Victor and he changed the subject right away.

Still, I got to have lunch with him and Emmylou at Kuleto's, a new Italian restaurant near the Powell Street turnaround. The three of us chatted over our pasta. Emmylou was rereading Graham Greene, and I had just read *Jazz* by Toni Morrison, who (with Fiona) I'd also just heard speak at the Masonic Auditorium. How luxurious to enjoy an expensive lunch with a superstar and discuss literature! Conversation flowed between Emmylou and myself. I mentioned that the Improv was closing soon and that I thought Nashville might be a logical place to relocate, since I wrote songs. Plus, two of my siblings and their partners lived there. I was too proud to come right out and ask Emmylou or Victor for help in the music biz, but I kind of thought they'd offer.

Instead, Emmylou asked, "Why Nashville?" She noted how much I appreciated the ocean, the weather, the multiculturalism that San Francisco offered but Nashville did not. "Why not continue to pursue music in San Francisco with its hearty roots-music scene instead of starting over somewhere new?" Victor nodded in agreement with the wise boss lady.

This was not what I wanted to hear. How could one-third of my musical trinity say such a thing? For the rest of the meal I behaved well enough, but my thinking broiled. *How dare she be so sensible! She just doesn't know how good I am.* Then my disappointment hardened into resentment. *Oh yeah, Emmylou? I accept your challenge. I will stagger you. I will conquer Nashville, just wait and see.*

The night of Western Electric's last show arrived. On the high stage at the Bottom of the Hill, I swayed to the left behind my mic in my Betsey Johnson skirt and boots. The club was packed. A little tipsy, I kept knocking my head against the low beam on the vaulted ceiling of the stage. Afterward, I celebrated the bittersweet occasion by drinking buckets of beer and telling anyone who would listen about my idea to move to Nashville. Ramona, the beautiful badass bar owner, kicked us out at 2 am.

In the final days before the Improv shuttered its faux-brick stage, I talked Mia and Fiona into going on a road trip with me. Invited or not, I had decided to move to Nashville. Once a big fish in a small pond at my rural Tennessee high school, I hoped favor would shine on me again, this time in Music City. Getting a job writing songs on Music Row seemed more logical than getting noticed for my songwriting in San Francisco. Besides, moving made me feel better, whether I walked or ran or drove. After I talked myself into this idea, it was all I could think about. Things would be better there. I enjoyed Victor's company plenty; I loved my siblings who lived in middle Tennessee; and Charlie had left LA and lived solely in Nashville these days.

    I sat on Mia's tan corduroy couch, where I had slept for a few nights since moving out of the shared apartment. My best friends were ready to roll with me, and I buzzed with excitement about what lay ahead. Fiona said she wanted to see more of the country—she had only ever lived in California—and could commit to a six-month trial someplace different and new. Mia was ready for adventure, too. She'd booked a flight out of Nashville to Thailand to visit her father. Buzzed from the bon-voyage drinks with the friends I'd be leaving behind, I opened the book of poetry that Chloe had given me to keep my heart beating strong on my travels. A fifty-dollar bill drifted out from between its pages.

Swollen Appetite

The next morning was cold and sunny when we met on Townsend Street in front of the Auto Driveaway garage. We wanted an early start and had arrived just before they unlocked their gates and rolled up the door. I had qualified to drive someone else's brand-new Toyota Celica from San Francisco to Birmingham, Alabama, which was less than three hours south of Nashville. We loaded the Celica to the gills with what was left of my possessions, a suitcase apiece for each of my pals, plus Nellie and her cat box. I'd made several mixtapes of our favorite singers: Maria McKee, Kristin Hersh, Kelly Willis, John Doe, Tori Amos, Victoria Williams. We took turns at the wheel.

The first night of our odyssey, the toilet backed up in our cruddy motel room in Needles, on the Arizona-California border. No big deal, said the man at the front desk, and we moved to another cruddy room. On the second day of driving, we pushed past good judgment and continued late into the night. We listened to doomsday preachers on AM radio to amuse ourselves and stay awake. The overstuffed car wound around dark curves and long stretches of nothing except for the occasional closed American Indian souvenir shop. Two lanes of desolate Highway 40 strained before me as we combed the moonless night for signs of life, or at least lodging. Out of nowhere, a white owl flew so close to the windshield, our eyes locked. We all three shrieked and I swerved off the road and just managed not to wreck the car. Clouds of dust rose in the pooled light of our high beams, and it took a while to calm down. Then I gunned the gas and lunged over the uneven pavement back onto the dark road. The local spirits were warning us, chasing us off their sacred land,

and we complied. When we found a motel room, we collapsed. We fell asleep as Nellie kicked litter against the plastic walls of her cat box.

The next morning, the third day of our drive, we discussed what had happened the night before over our various Denny's breakfasts: a vegetarian omelet for Mia, French toast with a side of bacon for Fiona, and a Moons Over My Hammy breakfast sandwich for me. It had simply been a white owl in white owl country last night, not a bad omen. We were educated, feminist women from a big city, after all. Nonetheless, a seed of doom germinated in my gut.

By the evening of the third day, we inched over the flat and spindly-pined Missouri line into Tennessee and stopped in Memphis. Not wanting to repeat the mistake we'd made the night before, we decided to hole up and leave the next day even though my brother and sister-in-law's house was four hours away in Goodlettsville. We checked into a room, bought a twelve-pack and some cigarettes, and thought about going to Graceland the next morning. None of us were Elvis fans, but the kitsch factor held great appeal. We noted with borderline hostility that Garth Brooks was playing the Memphis Pyramid stadium by the Mississippi River, so we'd better not go down there. We ordered pizza and left the motel room door open for ventilation while we waited for the delivery. A cloud of cigarette smoke hung in the humid air. Then a cockroach as long as a grown man's finger ran across the carpet, and we screamed. A security guard raced to our room and stomped it dead, then told us to keep it down, and winked. He asked if we were going to hold a funeral for the roach.

Swollen Appetite

The next morning we woke up excited to see our new town, so we skipped Graceland and headed east on I-40. We skirted the small but pretty Nashville skyline and cheered, then drove north on I-65 to Goodlettsville and up into my brother and sister-in-law's steep driveway. They welcomed the three of us into their home and made a big Southern dinner of baked ham, hot yeast rolls, and yellow squash casserole. Before delivering the car to its owners in Birmingham, we used it to go out and see the sights, take Mia to the airport, and look for an apartment. Then we washed the car and wiped down the interior, and were careful to remove all specks of cat litter, spilled coffee, and cigarette ash. Starved for Bay Area news and company, the young South Asian Toyota owner fed us delicious Indian food and gave us spices.

Chapter 12 - Dear Nashville, You're Someone Else's Dream

If you are trying to fall in love with Nashville, winter is not the best season to arrive. Having missed the majesty of fall, when the rolling hills are wigged in fiery red and flaxen leaves, like I had witnessed when I lived in rural Tennessee during my high school years, I tried to explain to my friend that sometimes it was pretty here. Now, shadows cast from the slender trunks of bare trees hatch-marked the hillsides studded in silvery dead grass. The bare branches of sycamores and cottonwoods stood at attention, like the crosses at Calvary, against a gray sky that skimmed the pewter-colored Cumberland River.

We found an apartment on Woodmont Boulevard near Granny White Pike. As a wet winter loomed over our colonial-style apartment building and the mid-century red-brick houses in our new neighborhood, and the thermometer dipped below freezing each night, it was good to have Fiona's company. She warmed me with encouragement to sing and write songs. She believed I had the goods and would find my place in the music scene.

Swollen Appetite

On the wall of our living room—a room devoid of furniture save a few pillows, a boombox, and a string of plastic, chameleon-shaped lights—Fiona and I tacked six hand-drawn calendar pages to a bare white wall: December through May. We'd agreed to give Nashville six months to win us over, after which we'd either have triumphed or go back to San Francisco. Each night we took turns crossing off another day with a thick black felt-tip marker before bed. Our nighty-night ritual.

My siblings who lived nearby helped us set up our apartment. They, too, believed in my talent and said I had a beautiful voice, having heard me sing in church, elementary school talent shows, and, later, high school garage bands. They lugged over odds-and-ends furniture, including two beds, dresser drawers, a small kitchen table, potted plants, and bags of groceries. Our laughter bounced off the walls as we clustered on the shiny hardwood floor of the still-empty living room, making sarcastic jokes and drinking beer while we ate takeout. Nellie curled into a ball in my sister's lap. A dark-humored bunch, we made light of our difficult childhoods in Florida and then Tennessee, like a group of veterans having a beer at the VA Hall. In my marrow, I knew my siblings loved me, and oh, how I had missed them during my years on the West Coast. But it had been well over a decade since we had lived near one another, and in the time apart, we had carved out very different lives. My siblings were on respectable, middle-class trajectories, while I had been living out by the Pacific Ocean, swinging by the seat of my pants.

To try Nashville after San Francisco seemingly made sense, since I was not just a singer but a songwriter as well. Proximity to my family would help ground me, help me accomplish what I wanted so much: to make a go of it as a musician. Singing made me feel like I could harness the Holy Ghost. Writing surprised and delighted me. But making a living as a musician had been much harder to do in San Francisco than I had expected. Maybe Nashville would be a better fit. I needed a new start to my new start. The boldness of my move to SF let me know I could shift gears and rise to the challenge of change. But I kept losing control. Family could help me feel like I belonged, and maybe Charlie or Victor would give me a piggyback ride to stardom.

Fiona and I explored our new neighborhood. Across a muddy patch of lawn that led to an undeveloped street, behind icy tennis courts and a dormant community rec room, we found a straight shot to booze, cigarettes, and pocket pies. Lingering autumn leaves skittered across the uneven pavement and birds chattered and trilled from treetops thick with mistletoe along Gale Lane. Red clay veined the ditches alongside the blacktop. When we passed S&M Communion Bread, the name made us giggle. From then on we mocked the white building with black window panes at every pass: *Good Catholics be eatin' the body of Christ, y'all.*

Once we understood the lay of the land, we ventured out daily into the gloom. I would rebound from my morning hangover by lunchtime, and just beyond the S&M building, a gut-bomb burger restaurant beckoned with its molded-plastic bright-orange booths and floor-to-ceiling windows that looked at the overpass maze where the Four-Forty Parkway, Franklin Pike, and Highway 65 intersected. We had to find liquor with a higher alcohol content than the 3.2% beer the nearby gas station and grocery store sold. Tennessee's blue laws segregated liquor and wine from beer. A package store sold the hard stuff a half mile down Franklin Pike, and just past that stood the Sutler Saloon, a great old bar with Western style swinging doors, sticky tabletops, and live music.

Because we did not have a car, we hoofed along the sidewalk-less blacktop, taking in the Nashville winter. Men with full gun racks on their muddy pickup trucks yelled weird shit. Fiona hid her middle finger behind the grocery bag she toted, and, once they were out of sight, I wagged my hips and said, "Hell yeah, I've still got it." Our boots shuffled on the pavement. Another dog in yet another yard barked and snarled and chased us well past their property line. We hugged the shoulder of the road, jumpy, God forbid we stray into someone's yard. We agreed the lack of leash laws was barbaric.

Our new neighbors claimed to welcome us when we slid into a booth at the Waffle House. A fellow patron would lean over and ask, "Where y'all from?" People held us hostage for the time it took to say any word with a vowel in it. Then they left us with their blessings, "Welcome to God's country y'all," even though we were in a city. Fiona thought they were friendly and sweet. I didn't trust them. Fiona told me I needed to be stronger, less afraid. She taught me how to fight, and how to fake out a perp by acting like you're about to punch him in the gut but instead swinging around to his lower back and punching him in the kidneys. Nellie sat in the window and watched us drink and act like fools in the spacious living room.

We learned the bus routes because we were bus riders. A few folks looked at us sideways, but most averted their eyes when we boarded to check out Nashville's downtown. In the city center, office workers milled around the federal buildings and insurance companies. The dingy and forgotten downtown had no pulse, not even in Printer's Alley. We took the bus to other places beyond walking distance, like the DMV, and out to the airport when Fiona's grandmother passed away and she went to the funeral in Nebraska. When she returned a few days later, dragging a duffel bag filled with a small black-and-white television and a few other items from her grandmother's house, I took the bus back to the airport to meet her. I listened to Nirvana on my Walkman and avoided engaging with the other passengers.

When people found out we were from San Francisco, and because Fiona wore an eyebrow ring, folks assumed we were gay. In many ways it worked to our advantage. For instance it weeded out the talkers. Very few women pierced their eyebrows or wore combat boots with dresses in 1993 Nashville. Someone made the joke our first week: "Women in Nashville put on their makeup before they get into the shower."

We complained about the apparent hypocrisy in the privacy of our apartment. We quoted the comedian Bill Hicks—"What you readin' fer?"—anytime one of us saw the other with a book, even the coloring book Fiona kept herself busy with at night while I drank one weak beer after another. It became clear that if you didn't listen to strangers ruminate about people you didn't know, you were considered rude. I didn't want to be rude; I just had so much to do. Award-winning songs needed me to write them, and a new band begged to be found. I was thirty years old, for chrissakes, without much time left, and I itched to prove myself instead of listening to someone tell me about that one time their cousin went to San Francisco.

I drank to quiet my restlessness and anxiety. "I drink because I think," a friend would say as he raised his glass. *Amen, brother.* Fiona had known I drank a lot, but since we hadn't lived together before, she did not know how much. Now, daily, she surrendered most of the six-pack to me and drank very little whiskey. I saw her sacrifice and was grateful. We had limited funds, and she said she didn't want more than a beer or two. I felt self-conscious until the third or fourth drink, when my attention shifted to counting what was left of our stash.

The accents, the fried food, the expectation that women act a certain way, the lack of openly gay folks, the segregation, so many white people, and the injection of Christianity into every aspect of society, including casual conversations with bank tellers and people in line at the grocery store, could not have been more unlike the proud and wild diversity of San Francisco. Walking home from a job interview, I saw a Latino man and waved at him. He looked down and crossed the street.

In preparation for our move, Fiona and I had rented the video *The Thing Called Love,* which is about Nashville's Bluebird Cafe and stars River Phoenix (his last film),

Samantha Mathis, Sandra Bullock, and Dermot Mulroney. We considered it a training film. To my surprise, I could walk to the Bluebird—two and a half miles in each direction was walking distance to someone who had lived in San Francisco—and so I applied for a waitress position. My work experience included fast-paced nightclubs, the Improv Comedy Club, and the Warfield. The Bluebird hired me on the spot. Yet something about the ease with which I got the job didn't sit right.

    I knew it hadn't hurt that I could name a well-connected reference. Victor was not thrilled that I had moved to his city, where his estranged wife and child lived, but he still made time to see me. He invited Fiona and me over to his house, and we drank Tennessee whiskey under the Christmas tree. He made a point of telling stories about how tenacious some songwriters were—their many attempts to get Emmylou to hear and hopefully record their songs. Even the expensive bottle of whiskey he continued to fill our glasses with had had a cassette tape inside the box it came in, and one clever songwriter had managed to load a Walkman player sent as a gift with a cassette. I got it: he would not be my song mule. At least he offered to be my job reference and drove us around to see the sights. He even took us to a few live shows at a cool nightclub, 3rd and Lindsley—where he dropped us off, not yet ready to be seen in public with me.

    How unassuming the Bluebird Cafe looked in real life! A small, one-story club at the end of a strip mall. Naturally, I fit right in as a budding singer-songwriter, and I hoped to make friends and find bandmates there. They served beer in cans. In the 1990s, cans of beer still had pull tabs. The nail on my right index finger bled and got infected from all that tab pulling. Musicians I admired poured in through the delivery door on a regular basis, either to perform or to watch the shows: Gillian Welch and David Rawlings, Rodney Crowell, Kevin Welch and Kelly Willis, Kieran Kane and Jamie O'Hara. Even Lucinda Williams was a regular. Coworkers introduced me to the musicians they knew, and I shoehorned in stories about the big stars I had met working at the Warfield: watching Dwight Yoakam's music documentary, *This Time*, being filmed, or moving chairs away from the mosh pit while Pearl Jam sound checked "Jeremy." I talked up my comedian connections as well—how David Spade had followed me around during my cleaning-woman duties in the condo where headliners stayed, then sat on the side of the bathtub wearing his mouthguard while I scrubbed the toilet. He asked for dating advice and my opinion about what women wanted. The people in God's country were easy to impress, and, again, I was suspicious.

Cold from walking home after work late one December night, I went straight to the kitchen to pour cheap bourbon into a glass. The coat I hung on the back of a kitchen chair smelled like woodsmoke. Nellie mewed and I scratched beneath her chin, which she stretched to impossible lengths. I popped the top off a bottle of weak beer, took my drinks back into the living room, and hunkered down on the floor across from Fiona. I held my bottle up to her and she held hers up to mine.

"How was work, Sandy?" she asked.

"Not terrible. Lucinda sat in my station tonight," I replied. "And the walk home was moonlit and beautiful. All the dogs were inside."

"Hmmm." Fiona tucked back into whatever she was writing, uninterested in my antics. I clicked the top of my ballpoint repeatedly as I let the liquor slide down my pipes and warm me up. My notebook beckoned. What kind of magic would unfold across these silky bare pages tonight? Would a journal entry lead to a new song lyric? I missed singing so bad it hurt. Want ate a hole through my middle.

Lucinda Williams and her bandmates had indeed sat in my station that night. I hovered over them and listened. Lucinda's songs could wipe the floor with those of any other alternative-country musician. Even her speaking voice weakened my knees with its strangeness and attitude. She ordered an Amstel Light. On and on, her crew belabored the merits of Townes Van Zandt's songwriting and how no one could compare except maybe Steve Earle. Again, I bristled at how musicians in Tennessee exalted one another to the point of worship. I preferred to shit-talk the competition. It seemed more honest than adulation, which smelled like ass kissing. I would not bend to fit in.

I thought, *You and I are kin, Lucinda Williams.* I sang country-rock in my last band in San Francisco, I'd written plenty of songs, and I dated Charlie, a man who sang harmonies on many of Lucinda's recordings and just so happened to live in Nashville. By my logic, dating a musician Lucinda had worked with made me her peer.

When we had first arrived in town, Charlie had met Fiona and me at a coffee shop near Vanderbilt University and told us which clubs to hit—the Exit/In, 12th & Porter, the Pub of Love, the Station Inn—and who played where. The Ryman was under construction, being renovated, and was scheduled to reopen the following summer.

    The next week, the three of us sat on the hardwood floor of our near-empty living room and drank a twelve-pack while Nellie napped in a sunny spot near the window. Every word Charlie said was meant for me. We stared at each other from across the room and had to work to include Fiona in the conversation. He said his upcoming European tour would make him more money than he ever made touring the States, so I mentioned that Victor had said that same thing about Emmylou, casually letting him know I was seeing Victor again. That's all it took. After Charlie heard about Victor, he tried to steal me away. Charlie said his fiancée had dumped him. For good this time. I swelled with my new status as a prize.

    Once he found out about the competition, Victor decided to take his chances on being seen in public with me. He pulled up to the apartment complex and I jumped into his Jeep. He drove to a movie theater on the outskirts of town and we got stoned in the parking lot before going in to watch *Wayne's World 2*. Too high to follow the plot, and because I asked more than once out loud, "What's going on?" Victor decided we should leave mid-movie. The next morning he offered to let me use his Jeep while he worked. I drove to a nearby park and hiked a cold and desolate but sunny trail to the top of a big hill. I sang as full-throated as I wanted but didn't dare to in our apartment. I sang a sad song, one written by Emmylou's ex-husband, Paul Kennerley, and Kelly Willis, "World without You." The mournful refrain rose from the soles of my feet, bounced off the bare hillsides, and blasted into the universe. I hoped a music producer might be out hiking, hear it, and discover me.

At the Bluebird, I made friends with some of my coworkers. In particular, one of the bartenders and I hit it off. Grace was a talented songwriter and a pretty, petite brunette. At closing time she and I stacked the wooden chairs on the tables, locked the doors, and turned out the lights. Then we lit a candle, kicked our feet up on the bar, and drank and complained about our men into the wee hours. Neither Charlie nor Victor spent enough time with me, and the bartender's guy, more famous than mine, wouldn't take her out in public, either. I worried that I was too wild for my country boys, and Grace thought she might be too old. Still, we both expected to win our guys over in the end. All those shots of Jack with Budweiser backs made the fire in my belly roar with resentment instead of inspiration, and I wrote petty gripes in my journal instead of song lyrics.

I made friends with another coworker, Lou. I'm pretty sure Lou wanted more than friendship, and I sort of tried not to encourage him. Thoughtful and inclusive, he took Fiona and me to parties and told us about upcoming shows and auditions. He went out of his way to drive us places. He told me about an audition call for backup singers for John Cougar Mellencamp and submitted a cassette of my best original material on my behalf. One of the songs,

I thought, showcased my outsider's perspective, "Banjo Ditty":

> *Sitting at a table see the dance floor swirl*
> *c'mon pretty baby won't you give me a twirl*
> *oh no, I can't hear the music*
> *I wish I knew then that I wouldn't know now*
> *that I could eat my cake and be happy   somehow*
> *oh no, I can't hear the music*
> *Everywhere I've been, well, I think I own*
> *and everyone I've touched, won't survive alone*
> *oh no, can't hear the music*
> *{slow to half time}*
> *...at a dance floor table I think and sit*
> *I have never known when it's time to quit*
> *oh no, I can't hear the music*

Lou took us to a party at Gillian Welch's house. (This was three years before her gorgeous debut album, *Revival*.) Turns out, she and Dave Rawlings had also moved to Nashville from California, she told us as she showed us around her mid-century home. We sifted through a stack of vintage fabrics she'd accumulated for various sewing projects, which interested Fiona more than me. When I offered Gillian a swig from my bottle of Jack Daniels, she politely declined, saying she didn't drink anymore, but thank you nonetheless. That didn't sit well with me. Seemed phony-baloney. I thought I knew what she meant. I had known a few people along the way who had gone through rehab, mostly comedians. Who got sober was almost as popular a topic as who was gay. Her declaration of sobriety touched a nerve, and when we left the party, I busted my empty whiskey bottle at the foot of her driveway. I hooted and laughed my ass off. That would show Ms. Sober Lady! But that was not before trying to lure Dave Rawlings into working with me on my songs and joining my nonexistent band.

Lou also took us to a party at Lucinda Williams's house on her fortieth birthday. A tanked Lucinda at one point locked herself in her bedroom. We partygoers did not leave, though. Lou played acoustic guitar and a handful of us sang songs, including The Byrds' "Down in the Easy Chair," hoping we'd get Lucinda's attention. But she never came out of her room, and we left just before dawn.

I woke up with a shitty dry mouth and realized a warm body was pressed next to mine. I rolled over, and there was Lou. *Oh, fuck no*, I thought. He smiled sweetly. Just like in San Francisco, I had gotten sloppy and tripped over my entanglements. I could not go very long without someone's arms around me. As soon as he skedaddled, Fiona came into the kitchen. I said, "No orange juice for Lou." Fiona shook her head.

Poor Lou thought it meant we were a proper couple, that our bond would last longer than a night. To me, that seemed downright stupid. I had to remind him I was already in more serious relationships with more important boyfriends. That hurt his feelings. He told everyone at the Bluebird about me dating more than one guy at a time. One of his friends wrote me a very terse letter. I pretended I didn't care what Lou thought or said about me, and from then on we ignored each other when we worked the same shifts. I did not want to play with trifling no-names, but still, I had lost a valuable ally. As much as I wanted to be a fuck-all-y'all person, the way regret hounded me suggested otherwise. *I didn't mean to hurt Lou,* I explained to coworkers, silently, in my head.

One morning in mid-January I woke up as usual, wincing and dehydrated, mortified at the memory of Fiona banging on my bedroom wall, telling me to stop singing in the middle of the night. I gently pushed Nellie aside and got out of bed. Every inch of my body ached on the way to the kitchen to get a cup of coffee. I tiptoed around Fiona until I could gauge just how sick of me she was. Then I soaked and shuddered in a hot bath, trying to relieve my hangover. I prayed, *please, please, please help me.* I made deals with whomever I prayed to, just as I made with Jesus as a little girl. *I'll be good, I promise.*

    I could not find purchase on Nashville soil. It didn't hold me upright. Neither of the men I wanted to love me or help me were cooperating. Tennessee did not feel like home. I was working at yet another nightclub, slinging drinks, and my songs did not feel like winners. One night when I came home from work, there sat Fiona on the floor of the living room, waiting for me with her back to the wall and legs splayed as she colored in her book. She showed me the picture she was working on of a freckled, blonde, curly-haired little girl holding an umbrella, with blue sky above and raindrops pouring down inside the umbrella. She had written above the scene, "Sandy is the saddest girl I know." It surprised me that Fiona saw me that way. I thought she saw me as a wildcat paying her dues and about to make it big. By candlelight, we solemnly crossed off another calendar square.

It snowed and sleeted often during the winter of 1994, so I called cabs to take me to work or for a quick supply run. Almost three months into living in Tennessee, I waited on the front steps of our red brick building, breathing in chimney smoke and burrowing deeper into my coat. The smell of wet dirt rose up from under the melting snow, and drops fell from the icicles in the eaves and left freezing trails beneath my scarf. Fixated on miserable thoughts, I didn't move out from under them. Yesterday morning on this same step, we'd found a dead bird—whole, beautiful, and frozen to the step.

It took less than twenty minutes round trip to and from the closest market. The cab driver let the meter run while I grabbed a six-pack and cigarettes, pork rinds and Hostess cupcakes. Back home, this weak beer kept me from pulling my hair out, but it did not inebriate. At work I would drink my fill after my shift with my bartender buddy Grace and let Fiona sleep.

Fiona and I wrote letters on bad-weather days, stuck in the apartment and sick of each other. Receiving a letter made my day, so I sent as many as I could to keep the exchanges going. Long-distance phone calls were expensive, so I allocated the few I could afford to calling my mother in Florida. Fiona corresponded with a slew of pen pals as well as keeping a very active journal. I wondered what she wrote about me but didn't dare look. While she scribbled away, I opened my notebook. I wanted a deep dive into something meaningful and rich. I needed to feel something besides panic and frustration. But no melodies or insights swept me away. I wrote Billy instead. Billy, my cherished Improv friend, a brother in arms and my lifeline to civilization. He charmed me with letters full of witty stories and clever cartoons he drew. He wrote often and kept me abreast of the San Francisco scene. He sent me a homemade papier-mâché heart attached via electrical tape to a painted black ruler. It became my scepter, this thickly painted, sticky-red heart. I sent him letters full of stories about the people I met and worked with and their strange customs.

Lousy weather and expensive cabs wore us out. We needed a car. I complained about it to my brother, and, wouldn't you know, his friend might be interested in selling his 1980s Mustang. My brother set up a visit.

The mint-condition Mustang must have been that guy's baby. He attached a few strings to the purchase, like relaying regular check-ins about its performance and letting him know when we got it serviced. He would not have sold it if my brother had not asked. And like it was a good luck charm, Fiona got a job that same week. She worked during the day and I worked at night, which made it easy to share the car. I drove home after work three sheets to the wind, weaving through neighborhoods to avoid the cops on the freeway.

A few weeks passed without incident, until I stayed up all night drinking, then called Charlie at dawn. It had been weeks since I'd seen him. The sun rose warm enough to melt the ground snow, making it a perfect day for a hike. I did my drunken best to beguile him into going with me. Seems like a good idea to get out of that stuffy studio and get some fresh air, right? Nature-wrought inspiration, I said, brings us closer to God. He said all that sounded great but it was crunch time. "I have to finish writing the lyrics for the last few songs on the album," he said. "I'm genuinely sorry but I can't go with you."

And that was that. I broke. I hung up on him and slid along the floor until my cheek flattened against the dirty hardwood, eye level with an overflowing ashtray. Tears and snot flowed across my face to the floor and I dragged my finger through the goo and cigarette ash. I was always fighting, fighting to get it right, fighting for someone's attention, fighting to prove I was special. *Why don't I matter? Doesn't he love me enough to drop what he's doing? Why is everything so hard?*

I picked up the phone and called my mom. Her response to how upset I was first thing in the morning sounded like genuine concern, not the anger or impatience I expected. "Sandra, go to bed. You'll feel better after you rest." The gentleness in her voice carried me to bed and I slept it off.

Not long after this ragged morning, the Northridge earthquake wreaked havoc near Los Angeles. From the couch in the community rec room, where the television reception was better than in our apartment, Fiona and I watched news clips of raging fires and crumbled buildings.

We were helpless as we watched California suffer. We sat, dumbfounded, in heated comfort in Nashville, guilty and worried for our friends and Fiona's family.

A few days after the earthquake, we walked through a grocery store, pushing a cart full of individual fruit pies wrapped in waxed paper (five for a dollar!), peanut butter, bananas, and, maybe, crackers and canned soup. I stopped mid-aisle and gave voice to what we had both been thinking.

"We could leave."

Fiona misunderstood at first. She thought I meant we could leave the grocery store. "We need food," she said in exasperation.

"No, not the grocery store. We could leave Tennessee. We could leave Tennessee and go home. We have a car, we're not happy here, let's just go."

And that is exactly what we did.

We went back to the apartment and rushed around as if we were about to get busted. We grabbed the cat and as much else as the Mustang could hold. We took the shower curtain down and wrapped it around some boxes on the ski racks on top of the car to protect them from the winter weather. We tied down the bundle as best as we could with clothesline. As we pulled away from the apartment complex, I dropped a check for the first car payment to my brother's friend in the big blue mailbox. We figured the deposit would cover the unpaid rent on the apartment. Then we got on I-40 and hauled ass west.

The Mustang's heater had given up the ghost, so we wore mittens and coats and hats inside the car. Below-freezing temperatures outside made the protective plastic shower curtain crack and blow away in chunks. We left a trail of frozen pieces of it along the highway. Pages blew out of the exposed boxes. So much for Fiona's journals and letters and my poems and songs. Whichever of us drove kept one hand on the steering wheel and the other tucked between her legs.

Dear Nashville,
You are someone else's dream.

Not until we needed gas did we get off the road at a truck stop in Arkansas, and a helpful trucker tightened the knots in the rope around what remained of the bundle on top of the car. We mixed coffee with hot chocolate at the AM/PM and drove in the wake of a semi because the heavy snow was playing tricks on my vision. When we couldn't stand the freezing temperatures any longer, we stopped in Oklahoma and found a mechanic who looked at our heater. An easy fix: he replaced the thermostat and sent us on our way without charging us a dime.

We took turns driving and listened to Liz Phair. *Exile in Guyville* felt right. We were done taking any shit. We were not cut out for country living and needed to get back to the city real bad. Finally warm, two days later, we crossed the Arizona border into California as a train rolled alongside us and blew its whistle. We had run out of things to talk about. With so little money between us, we did not stop as often as we should have. The roadside chaparral and sage blurred outside the passenger window, and at one point I could have sworn I saw Michael Jackson chasing a jackrabbit while Dead Can Dance droned from the cassette player. Some hallucinations leave marks. Fiona dozed as we bumped along and I could not stop thinking, *oh fuck, oh fuck, oh fuck, what now?*

I-40 turns into CA 58 after the Mojave Desert and leads to Interstate 5. Having driven across the country in the middle of the winter, our tired and wobbly Mustang groaned as we tried to keep up with the semis and other vehicles headed up the steep grade of Tehachapi Pass. Our fellow drivers gave us a wide berth. Once over the pass and on the flatter terrain of the Central Valley we gassed up, refilled our coffee and hot chocolate cups one last time, and faced the final four hours of our exodus. I vibrated, jacked on caffeine, sugar, and constant motion. Fiona looked ready to snap, at her wits' end. I had held back my favorite mixtape featuring Dwight Yoakam for the finish line because we both loved Dwight and he represented California country, not Tennessee country. Overzealous, I got the Mustang's speed up to eighty and Fiona lost her shit.

"Don't blow this thing up now! We're almost home!"

We needed to get the fuck out of that car.

Chapter 13 - Ashes in My Mouth

Back in San Francisco, we fell out of the car and staggered into the Mission. I parked the overtaxed Mustang across the street from Mission Dolores, within a block of Fiona's apartment at the corner of Landers and 16th Street, and left it to hiss and tick at the curb. The rush of sounds and smells flooded my winter-starved senses. Accordion music played in the distance, and my mouth watered from the smell of a sidewalk hot dog vendor grilling sweet onions in sizzling bacon fat. As tempting as it was, we did not stop there. Our car-cramped bodies unwound for the next three blocks as we walked to our beloved Pancho Villa Taqueria. More than anything about San Francisco, I missed Mission burritos. I needed to feel the heft of a warm chile relleno burrito wrapped in foil and nestled between chips and salsa. We took our food to go. Grease seeped through the brown paper bag, I am pretty sure in the shape of the Virgin Mary.

    Burrito secured under my wing, we stood in a trance, staring at the remarkable array of strong beer in the cooler of the K&D Market on 16th. That's where Billy stumbled across us. His mouth dropped open, and I shouted, "Surprise!" Yet as glad as I was to see him, I sagged against him in defeat. Billy hugged us both, said life had not been the same without us, and remarked that all of his Improv mates had run amok. Tired and demoralized, I choked up against his shoulder.

Wise beyond her years, Fiona had kept her apartment, and she and her roommates allowed me to stay in an empty third bedroom until its occupant returned from his travels. Careful not to cause any more trouble for Fiona, I tried to be an exceptional houseguest. I didn't have enough money left to drink enough to get sloppy, anyway.

Outside the curtained French doors of my borrowed bedroom, Fiona's fifteen-pound Maine Coon cat crouched and growled while Nellie hid under my bed. The Coon managed to sneak in one night while I went to the bathroom and attempted murder. I got in between the cats and tried to unscramble a tornado of claws and teeth and flying fur, but not before the Maine Coon bit and scratched me bloody. Fiona locked him in her room, then rushed me into the well-lit bathroom and poured rubbing alcohol over the wound. Rusty ribbons of bloody fluid streaked the sides of the sink. Fiona bandaged my arm and put me to bed.

The next morning, my swollen fingers and hand looked like a ballooned surgeon's glove. I went into the kitchen where Fiona's roommate and her boyfriend were frying eggs on the gas stove. I proudly waved my wounded arm, and they took me straight to SF General on Potrero, the old brick hospital for people without insurance. When it was my turn, the staff put me on a makeshift bed, a propped-up gurney, and a nurse plugged an IV into my good arm to bring down the swelling, infection, and fever.

Several ER doctors came by to admire my injuries, and I felt like an emergency room superstar. My wounds were more exotic than their typical gunshots, gangrene, and car accident injuries. An exotic loser.

Lost, and without a plan for the first time in my life, I felt really, truly sorry for myself. No big ideas redirected my attention. I dreaded my siblings' response to our abrupt departure and put off calling them for days. I had not been able to wait for the Tennessee spring to unfold. No picnics for us in Centennial Park beneath the Parthenon. The fragile beauty of dogwoods blooming would happen without us. Nor would we attend the Ryman's grand reopening. When I mustered the courage to pick up the phone, my brother's biggest beef was that we had taken advantage of his friend and driven off in the Mustang before we paid for it. My sister-in-law was pissed that we had taken advantage of my brother. I understood. Disappointed in myself, I knew I had acted badly.

"It's not easy to be me," I said, and my brother snorted.

My family had cleared out and cleaned up our apartment for us. I had not called anyone at the Bluebird to give notice there, either. *Fuck them*, I thought, but the truth of the matter was I didn't have the guts to apologize for my unprofessional behavior. A few months after returning to San Francisco, a paltry last check from the Bluebird arrived in the mail, forwarded from the Woodmont address, with a handwritten note on the back from the owner, Amy: "Don't rush to forward this. She ran out on us."

Dinged up and sallow, I turned thirty-one years old in the spring of 1994. My arm looked like a junkie's from the cat scratches, and my roots needed bleaching. I had to get my shit together, but how? Scared and anxious, I sold the Mustang for more than we'd bought it for and sent the former owner his payment in full. I hid my small profit from Fiona even though I knew she needed money just as much as I did. It took months to get a job—much longer than ever before. I could not find any want ads interesting enough to get me out the door. Billy found a few under-the-table shifts for me taking tickets and checking IDs at a small theater on Mason that paid just enough to buy cigarettes. Dana Gould was performing a one-man show and I was a fan. That and the free after-shift beers made it worth putting on my makeup.

Jolisa, my Warfield pal, took me under her clown-tattooed wing and got me a part-time job working for her sister at a pattern-making company way out on Townsend, past China Basin. Work started at seven in the morning in an old warehouse filled with art studios and workspaces. I trudged along the sleepy streets of the Mission as the birds began to chatter and acquired a nodding acquaintance with one of the guys from the band The Dwarves. Our schedules crisscrossed in front of the Kilowatt Bar—I headed east into the rising sun as he walked away from it.

Jolisa's sister invited us, her employees, to drink from lunchtime on, and the mini fridge in the studio was restocked every morning with beer. I liked that a lot. What I didn't like was how demanding and impatient my new boss grew as she drank. She belittled everyone, especially her little sister, my friend. As the day came to a close late one afternoon, I was ready to tell her to leave Jolisa alone when she targeted me instead. She criticized and demeaned the pattern I had just made, at her insistence, by tracing a pair of vintage riding jodhpurs. I told her that if she didn't like it, she could shove it up her ass. She chased me through the tight hallway and down two flights of stairs out of the building onto Townsend Street. She did not have to tell me not to come back.

Outside the unemployment office on the corner of Turk and Franklin I stood and smoked. Car exhaust and eucalyptus scented the air from nearby Jefferson Square Park, the same park where my gay friends said they no longer cruised because it had become too druggy and dangerous. I traded places on the concrete wall splattered with pigeon poop with other jobless deadbeats and made a minimum of eye contact or conversation. Butts from Kools, Mores, Winstons, Marlboros, and Swisher Sweets littered the ground.

    I read the want ads over coffee and carefully rationed the day's cigarettes. Some mornings I dressed for interviews. But most days I walked, unfettered by a schedule. I wandered and roamed. Sometimes I headed down Divisadero to Fulton and stared at the golden peaks of the University of San Francisco, or all the way out to the wooded and well-to-do Park Presidio, then two blocks over to the 38 Geary bus to ride west to the windmills at Ocean Beach. I sat on the sand or the seawall and stared at the endless ocean and prayed, *Please help me.* Then I got back on the Geary bus and chugged up to the de Young Museum and the Japanese Tea Garden, and looped around the Steinhart Aquarium inside the Academy of Sciences because that part was free. Often I got off the bus and went to stand in front of the octopus display, alone in a wall all by itself, and stared into the creature's human-like eyes. We were both stuck. I leaned over the railing near the large pool at the front of the building and stared at the albino alligator's back. Then I hopped back on the Geary bus and rode past the Kabuki Springs and Spa and sushi restaurants in Japantown, past the junkies and winos who listed on the sidewalks of the Tenderloin. Union Square held little appeal since I had no money to shop or drink or eat. But I went anyway, even though it hurt to look at the world spinning around just fine without me adding anything.

    I thought about borrowing a friend's handheld video camera and making a documentary about five random Geary bus regulars who would let me follow them into their apartments and throughout their no-doubt interesting and strange days. Sometimes when I was walking, I heard music. I heard my breath. I heard the heel of my boot against the sidewalk. Melodies materialized on top of the rhythm as I hiked up Fillmore Street to the top of Broadway and stared out at the ocean, wide-eyed, panting but upright. I wished for a lover who could share the awe I felt every single time I saw the towers of the Golden Gate Bridge rise above the mighty Pacific. Someone I could write this new song for. From that perch, I let the fog-wind blow my hair back and radiated to the great beyond, *Why not me?*

    Contrite, I wandered around the fancy houses in Pacific Heights. I walked faster than my thoughts could keep up with, my head busy but background noise to the breath, the furnace of muscles pumped full of blood and oxygen, my heart and lungs strong for a smoker. Hours of this wore me out. It made sawdust of the day and kept me out of Fiona's apartment and hair. What mattered at this point more than anything was: walking helped to stave off that inevitable first drink. I waited as long as I could to take my medicine. Once a drink slid down my throat, I didn't know what I might do.

Fiona's roommate returned from his travels and I surrendered his room. Mia had returned from Thailand, and she and the two sisters she shared a flat with on Fell Street offered me a large closet to rent for very little money. Not uncommon, this tiny of a living space in San Francisco. It accommodated a twin mattress, a boombox, my suitcase, and the cat box. I had a small window that opened onto the tight space between the Victorian apartment buildings, from which I could almost see the sky. The guy in the apartment an arm's length away played REO Speedwagon late into the night. I yelled and banged on the wall to no avail. I countered his 1980s rock by playing Kristin Hersh, Freakwater, and Diamanda Galás even louder.

Four women and five cats lived in that three-bedroom flat. Familiar with the apartment from all the after-work gatherings and regular backyard barbeques of the Improv clan, it felt like a reunion at first. There was a big garden where Mia grew herbs and vegetables; she scattered orange and lemon peels over the dark soil to keep the cats from pooping in the plants. The women appreciated food and loved to cook. On the tiled kitchen counter, a pink sourdough starter grew under a dish towel beside the wooden vegetable bowl always full of fresh garlic, tomatoes, onions, limes, and avocados. Mia prepared pasta with sautéed garlic and olive oil, broccoli, tomatoes, and fresh basil from the garden, with a sprinkle of freshly grated parmesan and pine nuts. That dish, in particular, made life a little more bearable.

Less than a year earlier I had stood and felt an equal—someone with a raucous-bright future—among this group of women in front of the same television set, toasting Bill Clinton with shots of Bushmills as he was sworn into office. Before the inauguration we piled into someone's late-1980s Honda and drove to the sole Trader Joe's in the Bay Area, just over the Golden Gate Bridge in San Rafael. In traffic on the way back, we talked shit about the women there who wore diamond tennis bracelets and drove BMWs. If any of us had that kind of money, we'd talk about art and civil rights, not stocks or nannies. Into the tiny trunk we crammed our purchases of bulk walnuts and olive oil. A wine box filled with bottles of two-buck chuck, Bushmills, and cheap vodka rested on each lap. To celebrate like we had then seemed like a luxury now, an extravagant thing people who were winning got to do.

Having a place to get my bearings helped, and I was grateful to my roommates for the cheap rent, but the fire in my belly had grown cold. We did not hang out and party the way we once had, and I felt like a burden. Unmoored. I was a freeloader. And all my worldly belongings, including my body, fit into a closet.

I asked Fiona if I could take her to lunch at the Nordstrom's café downtown to thank her for her support in Tennessee and afterward. I could charge the lunch on my one credit card, a Nordstrom's card. We walked down Market Street, past the endless chess games played in the mall above the Powell Street BART station and in front of Payless Shoes. Pigeons waddled around the players and newsstands, where all of the various papers bore the same headline: "Kurt Cobain Found Dead in Seattle." Stunned, Fiona dropped a quarter into the newspaper box and each of us pulled out a paper. How could the biggest rock star on the planet have killed himself at twenty-seven!? He had been dead for three whole days before they discovered his corpse!

It was obvious that it was too late for me to become a famous singer-songwriter. *Joke's on me.* If I had behaved better in Nashville and kept at least one of those musician relationships, or had stayed married to Brad, by now I might live in a fancy house in LA and maybe even have a kid or two. But no, I'd run off to discover my art and failed. I would end up a crusty old truck-stop waitress, playing the jukebox and telling anyone who could decipher my slurring, *I could have been someone.* We ditched lunch, walked to Dalva, and played Nirvana on their jukebox the rest of the afternoon.

One quiet morning, in the midst of my post-Nashville unemployment, I sank into the well-worn tan corduroy couch and stared at the phone. After a few moments, I picked up the receiver and pressed ten buttons branded into my memory: Charlie's phone number. When he answered, I couldn't speak, but a whimper escaped my mouth. He knew my voice and tried to soothe me.

"I hope you didn't move to Nashville for me," he said.

"Of course I did," I confessed.

"Can you forgive me for not being who you wanted?" he asked.

I hated that he said that, as the last strands of hope broke.

I said, "Can you forgive stupid me?"

"You are many things, but stupid is not one of them," he replied.

I held the phone close to my ear, eyes full of tears listening to his Southern drawl speaking to me and only me for the very last time.

Not long after that call, I got into an argument at a backyard barbecue on Capp Street with a guy I had gone on a few dates with. I left the party in a dramatic huff, off my nut and murderous. Much later I came to from a blackout on Mission Street. Two women I didn't know were holding me up by my armpits as my feet stumbled along the sidewalk. I asked them where we were going, and they laughed and said, "*Coka*. We get you some *coka*."

I realized they meant cocaine and figured they must be sex workers. Never mind how kind they'd been to pick me up from wherever they had found me, I didn't want any *coka*—not, at least, from their pimp. I took off.

I wound my way back through the Mission, up 16th to Fiona's flat, and rang the buzzer again and again. I shouted her name from the sidewalk below her window. I agonized there for a few minutes, and when she didn't answer, I found a nearby pay phone and dialed the Fell Street apartment. Mia answered. She told me later that that call frightened her. She had not realized how messed up I'd become. She said she knew I could be sensational and wild, and that we all drank too much, but she thought nothing could harm me because my drunk aura was my superpower. I don't remember what I said on that call, but I do remember the trek ending at the corner of 12th Street and South Van Ness near Market, where I crumpled against the side of a building and watched the light crawl over the horizon.

Out of everyone's sight, I wailed, "What's wrong with me?"

Such a ragged pile of awful my life had become. I passed out for a while until rush-hour traffic and the merciful coos of mourning doves woke me.

Dear Hole in My Soul,
Please finish the job. Swallow the rest of me.

Chapter 14 - Gave Directions to Keanu Reeves

What happened when I drank wasn't right. I fretted on the twin bed in the closet room. My gut, my head, and my side hurt from having passed out on the sidewalk on Van Ness. Fear colored every thought that dread had not stained. I kicked off my boots and scooted far under the covers and pulled the blanket over my head. Nellie crawled in and curled up against my belly. I moaned and tried to fall back asleep but worry and daylight kept me awake. Booze was the sole relief I had. I decided it was time to stop. At the very least I had to moderate myself, because no way in hell was I giving up wine. Tequila, vodka, and bourbon would be for special occasions only. When my financial circumstances changed, I wouldn't have to drink so much. My attention turned toward getting help. Help from a man to take care of me so I wouldn't need to drink so much to feel better. Good thing that just a few weeks earlier, I had started dating a rising star.

I had stayed in contact with my ex-husband, Brad, all this time, even during my stint in Nashville. Not too close and not too chummy, but still, we kept in semi-regular contact. I did not tell him about my difficulties, only my victories. We liked each other and competed. Determined to out-cool him, I painted a debauched yet celebratory picture of myself so he could see how daring I'd become. I wanted him good and scandalized. As friends do, we sent each other mixtapes of new music and even hung out when his agent duties brought him up to the Bay Area. At the beginning of my post-Nashville funk, when I was still living at Fiona's apartment, he sent me a tape of a new musician he thought I would like. Touted as the new Dylan, the songs dangled like carrots and woke up my hungry rabbit. I needed a win and I accepted what felt like an unspoken challenge. Besides, the songs grabbed me with their rueful, unrealized-longing lyrics. This guy used his hurt to push his songs, and his voice soared and flagged with enough despairing beauty to stir the dead leaves smothering my self-esteem.

Guess who wanted to soothe the sad man's brow? Guess whose name I saw listed in the Pink Pages for a show at the Bottom of the Hill?

Keith, a clean-cut, Midwestern singer-songwriter, and I got together the night of the show. Thoughtful and funny, we proceeded to spend the next two weeks apartment sitting and getting to know each other in an almost yuppie part of San Francisco called Russian Hill, near North Beach. We rented a car and drove south and stayed with hip friends of mine who lived in Los Angeles, where he played a few solo acoustic gigs, and we palled around Melrose. I made sure Brad knew about us. Then we drove back up the stick-straight I-5 to San Francisco and apartment-sat some more. What a relief to feel light again!

To feel attractive and able to make someone happy. Even when his rental car got towed and I felt like it was my fault for not reading the street signs, he said it just gave us more time together. We perked each other up and began what became a very sweet relationship. When Keith left, he said he would call soon.

I stayed unemployed for six more agonizing weeks, spending hours at a time in bed not sleeping. Then I was hired to a union job at the French and Asian fusion restaurant Elka, in the Miyako Hotel in Japantown, even though a small piece of tissue was still stuck to my forehead when I interviewed with the general manager. (It took twenty minutes of fast walking to get to Japantown from the Fell Street flat, and I had built up a sweat that required blotting.) Working as a hostess at a restaurant that finicky food critic Michael Bauer endorsed also boosted my sunken spirits. I received health insurance and paid holidays for the first time in my life. I earned side money by waitressing part time at another new restaurant up in swanky Pacific Heights, the Alta Vista, and, later, LuLu's when it opened in a gentrified stretch of Folsom Street. It was 1994, and there were lots of shiny new restaurants. Even if I couldn't afford to eat at any of them, I would be fed employee meals since I was on staff.

  A slew of steady work made it possible for me to rent my very own studio apartment at 733 Fillmore Street. It was a good spot to perch—less than a block from Mia and the sisters, and Billy as well, with Hayes Valley two blocks down the hill and Japantown, the Lower Haight, and the Mission still within walking distance. Best of all, it was just a block away from my beloved Alamo Square. Daily, in between shifts, I sprinted up the steep steps on Fulton Street to climb to the crest of the park and the swing set, situated under massive redwood trees and near a tennis court built in the 1920s. At sunset, the wind picked up big and blustering on that peak and blew my hair into my cigarette, and the smell of burned hair mingled with that of smoke, redwood trees, and fog. My happiest of scents. Swaying on the durable cloth seat of the swing, I lightly dragged my feet one yard forward, then one yard back, as I smoked and stared at the iconic pastel Painted Ladies and the tourists lined up to take their pictures in front of them. My fantasy life stirred. Ideas for new songs and poetry started to bud like flowers in spring.

 I had bounced back from the Nashville debacle and made a concerted effort to moderate my drinking. One reason to keep it together compelled me more than ever: Keith and I spoke every few days on the phone, and his music was receiving scads of airplay. I needed to look good to keep getting invited along. Working breakfast and lunch shifts rather than dinner kept me from going out after work as often.

 My new studio apartment was decorated on a budget. With a Circuit City credit card I bought a nineteen-inch television set with a VCR in its base from their store on Van Ness. I set the TV on a cardboard box covered in a vintage tablecloth and positioned my one Salvation Army chair a yard in front of it. Nellie fell asleep in my lap, and one half of the allocated 1.5L bottle of Robert Mondavi cabernet was still in that bottle by the time I called it a night. Progress. Some nights I made it all the way through a film without passing out. I begged the universe not to make Nellie pay for the sins of her mother, to not let her get kitty lung cancer from my secondhand cigarette smoke.

Dear Nellie,

I'm not angry with you for burying my dirty underwear in your cat box when I went to LA for a week with my new boyfriend.

A boring but somewhat beneficial routine developed: after work, I dropped off my dry cleaning at the corner Chinese laundry, then picked up something to drink with dinner, and then Nellie and I sat in front of the television or I spoke on the phone with Keith. He lived in New York, but his new CD kept him on the road. I accompanied him on his California dates and referred to myself as Miss California. A title I had gotten used to. There were other women in other ports, but in California he was mine. He played the Warfield with Shawn Colvin, then started opening for Sheryl Crow on the West Coast leg of her tour. We stayed at the historic Roosevelt Hotel on Hollywood Boulevard with its Spanish colonial architecture and view of the Walk of Fame and Grauman's Chinese Theatre across the street. In San Francisco he stayed at the Phoenix or with me. (New boyfriend, new doorman.) We rode on Sheryl Crow's tour bus, and I laughed at the crew's jokes and gossip even though I thought they were misogynist and stupid. They referred to Sheryl's boyfriend as "Mr. Crow" behind his back because he walked her dog. They said that Lisa

Germano's songs were not songs or poetry but just plain weird. *Hmph, these guys are easily intimidated by strong women,* I thought.

As usual, whenever Keith and crew left town, I picked up the abandoned pieces of my life from where I'd dropped them when he arrived. I deflated after work at home in my studio with Nellie, just me and my cat. I ate dried-out leftover banquet food at work and beans and rice at home. I tried to find a local band but nothing jumped out from the pages of the *Bay Guardian*. Somehow I managed to get a date with local musician Chris Von Sneidern. We met at Record Finder on Noe Street and flipped through the bins. I mentioned I'd love to cover the Bad Company song "All Right Now," not in an ironic way but with full-throated redneck gusto, and Chris scoffed at the song choice. His mockery did not deter me, and I called him three sheets to the wind one night later that week. He said it was irresponsible of me to call him when I was tanked and try to seduce him. "What if I was a serial killer?" he asked. I decided he was mean and that this was his way of trying to get out of a second date.

Thoughtful and sweet, Keith called often. I lived for these calls. I'd say something clever, like "whatcha doin'?" and he'd say something sophisticated, like "trimming my toenails." Since I could hear the clippers in the background, it seemed like I had a real boyfriend on my hands. For the length of the call or the visit, anyway. I would have loved to be his one and only but was too cynical to ask for that. Besides, we had a chummy kind of love.

I remained semi-stable but stalled out as an artist. Dull and preoccupied with others. I read Leonard Cohen's esoteric novel *Beautiful Losers* for inspiration. Nellie and I watched the neighborhood cats roam the overgrown yards of the neighboring 1920s apartment buildings. With his songs on regular rotation on MTV, I worried that Keith would become too famous for me. Some guy at one of Mia's parties who had recently been at a party in Brooklyn with Keith ratted him out, told me he had brought a gorgeous woman to that party. *Asshole*, I thought—about the guy who told me that. I whipped up an impressive poem and song tout suite, along with a pornographic letter. The next time I spoke to Keith on the phone, I said he must find me and my ho-hum life pretty damn dull. He assured me that I was anything but boring, yet we continued to make no demands of each other when it came to fidelity.

When Victor came to San Francisco with Emmylou for a show at the Lesher Center for the Arts in Walnut Creek, I was lonely no more for one long weekend. What a hinky bond we had! Here he was, again, just like the Dolly song. I rode in a limo with Victor from San Francisco to Walnut Creek, and when the limo driver's son asked me for my autograph, I did not let him down by telling the truth: that he'd mistaken me for someone famous. Later that night, I asked Victor why, after all that had happened between us, he still wanted to see me. He said, "Because you're a babe." That made me feel better. Neither of us questioned why I wanted to see him.

And then, both Victor and Keith drifted away to live their exciting lives elsewhere. I did not anticipate seeing either of them again too soon. And this time, I did not care. I was weary. Sick of them both. Neither gave me what I wanted. I looked for another band in San Francisco. When a former bandmate from Western Electric asked if I wanted to work on a new music project with him, it felt like the tides were turning. We called our band Cornbag. We played original songs that we both wrote along with a variety of off-the-beaten-path country and soul numbers. We were eclectic and weird but pretty good, and had a great time rehearsing. He was married to a comedian who had landed a very successful nationally televised commercial, and they made a cool couple. I respected and admired their marriage. He listened to me kvetch about my lame love life and told me funny stories about various voice-over gigs he'd taken. I took the N-Judah, the aboveground Muni train, to my new bandmate's house and explored a new neighborhood, the Inner Sunset, with its tightly packed houses and cute little shops bordering a side of Golden Gate Park I didn't yet know. It felt good to establish deeper San Francisco roots. I belonged here, I fit in. Maybe I could still grow into the kind of artist that suited me instead of just being someone else's snack meat. We played a few shows, but then, after a few months, my bandmate decided Cornbag was not the right vehicle for him.

That knocked the wind out of my sails. I couldn't understand why he didn't want to work with me. A few nights after we skidded to a stop, I called him in a blackout. What I said must have been bad, because a few days later when I ran into his comedian wife on my way home from work in Japantown she shook her head in disappointment and gave me the what-for. She said I was too smart to act that way and should know better. I stood on the street and took it. Guilty as hell. I wanted her to tell me what I had done—the exact transgression that had pissed them off—but I feared what I might have said more than her wrath.

  Night after night I trudged home along that same route through Webster Square and down Fillmore Street, carrying my usual booty: a VHS movie and a liter of wine. One night not long after Cornbag broke up, a group of preteen girls swarmed me as I unlocked the outside door to my building and pushed me into the vestibule. The biggest girl demanded to be taken to my apartment. I said no, and she shoved me down to the floor and grabbed my bottle of wine along with a handful of my hair. The other girls shrieked and ran. I sat on the gritty concrete lobby floor feeling stupid and old. My head hurt, my heart thudded, and my scalp bled.

  Around this time I began to taste metal. I thought it must be the old plumbing in my turn-of-the-century apartment building, and that I was being poisoned with lead or mercury. Someone told me that adrenaline tastes like pennies. Panic was coursing through me in telltale ways, and it took a lot of wine to dilute its flavor. Music and wine continued to solve my emotional problems. Sort of. The American Music Club, Lisa Germano, and Hole were my go-to CDs at this apartment. And, of course, the albums Keith recorded. I listened to Lisa's strange meanderings of speak-singing and haunted violin playing in the mornings before work, then MTV after dinner, and the American Music Club lulled me into a sweet stupor with its tender hooks before sleep. And yet, as beautiful as Mark Eitzel's voice and Bruce Kaphan's pedal steel sounded, their music worked me up. American Music Club loosened the lid on my bottled-up crazy and fury found its way out of my mouth as I growled and hissed along with Courtney Love for the finish. Later I'd wind down, but not before my neighbor pounded on the ceiling.

One night, this neighbor walked right into my apartment and demanded I shut the fuck up. I must have forgotten to lock my door after smuggling a bag of empty bottles to the recycling bins of the apartment building next door. Or I'd arrived home after a show or dinner too wasted to remember to lock the door. He demanded I stop scream-singing and turn my obnoxious music down. Then he implored me, begged me to take pity on him and let him sleep—he had work in the morning for chrissakes, like normal people. Shocked and outraged that he didn't realize I worked in the morning as well, I told him to get the hell out of my apartment and go masturbate if he couldn't sleep. That's what worked for me.

I struggled to maintain my initial enthusiasm for my newish union job; the six o'clock start time for this nightly drinker in her early thirties sucked. It took tremendous effort. Good thing for my liver, vanity served me better than the insanity of my drinking and pushed me to scrimp by with a tall Asahi and airplane-size bottle of Grand Marnier on nights before the 5 am alarm went off. And if that small dose of alcohol didn't quiet me down, sleeping pills helped.

Each breakfast shift I left my studio apartment by half-past five and clacked along a dark Fillmore Street in my sensible low-heeled pumps, past the closed convenient stores and barbecue restaurants of the Western Addition, dodging rats and the new scourge of drug addicts known as crackheads who would not settle down before the sun rose. That shit scared me. It turned those poor fuckers into wind-up-toy zombies. I cut across the Safeway parking lot to McAllister, took the overhead pass above Geary into Japantown, and headed up Post Street to the basement employee entrance. I rode the elevator up to the dim restaurant bar, turned the lights on, chose a Muzak channel, and checked with the waitstaff to make sure their stations were up and running. I drank massive amounts of French roast coffee and stood at my hostess stand waiting to greet and seat patrons.

I made mellow mixtapes for work. Ones I thought could pass as pleasant and nonintrusive. I clicked a tape full of songs by David Sylvian, Maria McKee, Nothing but the Girl, and my main man, Nick Cave, into the cassette player in the Muzak closet, then watched one of my coworkers, a Jamaican man in his mid-fifties and a lifelong union worker, transfixed under a speaker in the bar area. He swayed and sang softly along with Nick Cave's cover of "By the Time I Get to Phoenix" while balancing a tray full of dirty coffee cups and saucers.

When my job at the Miyako began in 1994, the Japanese-owned hotel required female employees to wear skirts with hose and heels. Pants were not allowed. Those early-morning walks were cold. Thank goodness the hotel sold to Radisson not long after I started, and we could wear slacks and be motivated by corporate slogans like "If you think somebody needs to do something, remember you're somebody." These inspiring words hung on a placard above the time clock. *Fuck you, Radisson.* The somebody I still hoped to become had little to do with working at a hotel chain.

Slightly nicer than the average hotel in The City, the Miyako housed many of the artists that performed at the Fillmore and at another iconic concert venue, the Winterland, back when it had been open. With its traditional Japanese-style wooden tubs, rice-paper screens, and low tables with floor cushions in the pricier suites, it drew touring bands seeking a taste of the exotic. The City's significant music history for many people meant the Grateful Dead, Jefferson Airplane, and other hippie slop, but for me, the most memorable connection between the hotel and touring bands happened when the Sex Pistols stayed at the Miyako after playing Winterland on their first US tour. Not recognizing him, the doormen at the Miyako denied a very drunk and belligerent Johnny Rotten his room after the show. That had been some kind of last straw for Johnny Rotten; the Sex Pistols broke up two weeks later.

I worked at the Miyako from 1994 through 1998, and during that time I rode in an elevator with Debbie Harry; told Patti Smith I had not seen Todd Rundgren come through the lobby; got wasabi packets for Carlene Carter and Advil for Iris Dement; made a cappuccino for Adam Ant; gave directions to Keanu Reeves; watched David Byrne circle the lobby on his bicycle; seated Anthony Kiedis, Bonnie Franklin, Maya Angelou, Glide Memorial minister Cecil Williams, Governor Jerry Brown, and renowned Buddhist guru Robert Thurman; and ran Jean-Luc Ponty's MasterCard. In 1997, Tom Petty and the Heartbreakers stayed for a month when they played twenty sold-out shows at the Fillmore. I overheard them each day as they passed by the hostess stand on their way in and out of the hotel, their big celebrity heads bobbing on their skinny rock 'n' roll necks. They bitched and moaned and gossiped about something or other at every pass. It made me downright giddy to realize they were no better or more interesting than me! I liked to bitch and moan and gossip with my friends, as well as with my mid-tier major-label boyfriends and their crews. The comedians I knew and hung out with liked to talk smack.

From that same hostess stand, uniformed in professional black slacks and a mandarin-collared teal jacket, I watched a press conference with Jim Kerr from Simple Minds, and, a year later, a press conference with Jim Jarmusch for the film *Dead Man*. The rotating cast of musicians, authors, actors, and politicians that populated my new workplace brought much-needed verve to my life that my Salvation Army–furnished studio did not. I was born to direct celebrity traffic. It also provided me with scads of names to drop. One day I hoped one of those famous people would take me by the hand and walk me along the road to glory.

> Dear Fame,
> I'm right over here at the hostess stand.

Chapter 15 – Arrangements

After a year of working at the Miyako, the restaurant changed from Elka to a less fussy one named YoYo Bistro. The upstairs lounge and bar area where my hostess station stood was remodeled, and they added a small, exposed kitchen between my station and the bar, which served small plates and appetizers. I stood at my podium and chitchatted with the food prep guys in the late afternoons before happy hour and the dinner rush. I learned a little Spanish, and once made a prep cook blush when I asked him what the lyrics to the song "Besame Mucho" meant, since I sang it all the time without knowing. It means "kiss me harder," he said with a modest grin. The Vietnamese prep cook taught me how to cut burdock root and mangos, and always gave me the mango stones so I could gnaw away at the golden flesh still clinging to their sides. He also taught me how to make floating islands, a fluffy French-Vietnamese dessert with islands of meringue floating in a pool of vanilla tapioca with crème anglaise drizzled over the top.

Afternoons were sweet. I was no longer hungover, and my first drink of the day was not too far off. My cassette tapes played unobtrusively in the background until it was time to turn the Muzak station to soft jazz. I answered the phone, which rang a few times with calls for dinner reservations during the quietest time of the workday, the last part of my shift. Soon I could head home to my allotted number of drinks, eat some ramen, and watch a video with Nellie. During those hours, as the guys prepped food in the small kitchen, I worked on song lyrics a few feet away, amassing a pile of songs and little stories. It lifted my sagging spirits to write when I wasn't drinking. My words and creations glowed like electric-green heat lightning against a stormy future as strange rhymes shimmied down the lead of my pencil to the page. Sometimes I read a few stanzas to my co-hostesses or the guys in the kitchen. They were so easy to shock, I couldn't help myself.

I was ready to sing again. I wanted to sing *my* songs—put all these new lyrics written at the hostess stand to music. Via the *Bay Guardian* I found a couple of guys: a guitarist from Berkeley, Buck, who had curly brown hair and wore T-shirts and Levi's with Nikes, and another guitarist from San Francisco, Jay, who had a retro vibe in his 1960s plaid wool mackinaw, short black hair, and black-framed glasses. We started working on original music together. Buck, Jay, and I conjured up rootsy rock with a bold streak of outlaw country. In between the originals, written by either Buck or myself, we peppered the set with eclectic covers by the Stones ("Dear Doctor"), Waylon

("Lonesome, On'ry and Mean"), and for a touch of country-glam, Bowie's "Moonage Daydream."

We sometimes rehearsed at Jay's apartment in San Francisco's Outer Mission, at the precipice of a steep hill on Precita Avenue, a few blocks above the El Rio bar. I took smoke breaks at a pretty little park that offered a great view of the Mission unfurling into South San Francisco—all the tiny boxes on the hillside as far as the eye could see, or at least to Daly City. I smoked and watched the airplanes take off and land at SFO. Back at practice on the guitarist's pine-needle-covered patio, I plugged my mic cord into a guitar amp to get the desired raunchy, distorted, mid-1990s rock sound and we ran through Nick Drake songs for the hell of it. Distorted, dreamy folk stuff appealed to me. But the blues streak running through Jay's style made me uncomfortable.

More often we rehearsed in the godforsaken East Bay, namely Berkeley. I either caught a ride with the SF guitarist over the bridge or took BART from the 16th Street station. On its best day, the BART station stank of dried puke and decades-old urine. The Ashby station had its own specific quirks: if you needed a stolen car stereo, an area rug woven with the likeness of Jimi Hendrix or Jerry Garcia, or a green, red, and yellow Jamaican knit hat, you could find it there. During the brisk walk from the station to rehearsal, I aired out my hair with a quick smoke. A poster of Janis Joplin hung in the window of one apartment building I passed, and in the next yard, overgrown bushes obscured a sculpture made from wine bottles. ONE LOVE was spray-painted in fluorescent orange across the sidewalk. Buck's home, which he shared with another musician, smelled like watered-down Dr. Bronner's soap, brewer's yeast, and skunky old marijuana. The towels did not smell like they were laundered with enough detergent. Buck talked about "peaking" during his solos-turned-jam-sessions. But because his musical range included X, Kristin Hersh, and the Velvet Underground, I learned to tolerate his passion for Jerry Garcia.

The two guitarists struggled to find common ground stylistically, but I appreciated the attention they paid me. More than once, Jay picked me up in his vintage Buick and we drove out to Ocean Beach to catch the sunset and talk, not always about music. Same with Buck—we'd get something to eat and talk about literature and film, just the two of us. One night I confided in Buck that I feared I had a drinking problem and started to cry. Buck comforted me, and the hug led to us sleeping together. I appreciated being comforted, and sex was my thank you. When I told Jay I'd slept with Buck, he became angry with me. Between our stylistic differences and me "siding" with Buck, Jay quit the band. Buck and I forged ahead.

My musical life folded into my sex life. We did not act like a couple because Buck dated another woman, and he knew full well that the second one of my long-distance guys came through town, I would drop everything to see him. But his wicked laugh, quick wit, and Lou Reed–like voice kept me interested. It turned out I liked him a lot—this first Deadhead I had gotten to know. We partnered without a lot of fuss, romance, or tenderness. We were bandmates first and foremost.

Late one night I called Buck and railed into him about getting an HIV test. If he had HIV, I threatened, I'd leave him. I don't remember this call very well, but I do know that it upset Buck. He insisted he was low risk and worried that I would dump the band as well as the relationship. When we spoke the next day, him shaken and explaining that I'd sounded like a different person, I said, "I'm sorry. You're not the only one I've called wasted. Please dump me if I ever do that to you again."

    We kept going. Two of Buck's former bandmates joined us on bass and drums, and the four of us rehearsed often, for months. I enjoyed hearing my voice amplified with plenty of reverb over a PA in Buck's garage studio. Well aware of how messy I could get, I tried to own it, go with it, make it part of my shtick by wearing a T-shirt I'd altered with a Sharpie to blacken out the "o" in "country" to make it read "cuntry." A nod to Carlene Carter for her line about putting the cunt back into country music. We booked shows at Hamburger Mary's South of Market, the Bison on Telegraph, and open-mic night at Berkeley's Freight and Salvage.

    As the group's lone alt-country artist, I felt like the odd man out but kept it to myself because the others had hippie chemistry and seemed to enjoy the music we made. But I became frustrated at our rehearsals with my inability to express what I wanted to hear, musically. When we had disagreements about direction, I caved. I let Buck play how he preferred and then resented him for it. In his garage, slinky on the mic stand, with a beer in my hand and more in a cooler, I sang his songs or harmonized on his leads. Which were lovely, but not mine. When we did play my songs, he changed the arrangements to suit his guitar style even though I had recorded demos with other players doing arrangements I preferred. I understood wanting to make something one's own; to do otherwise stifles creativity. But when Buck rearranged the songs, he also took writing credit. And I let him because it no longer felt like mine or sounded the way I heard it in my head. *Oh, who gives a fuck? It's good to be working on music of any kind. Have another beer and let's get this show over with.* My baby creations were abandoned, and so they withered.

    Still, I wondered, why didn't Buck worship me? As we spent more and more time together, my feelings changed. We seemed like a couple now, not just friends who slept together. I watched Buck put together a bookshelf in his room and begin to arrange a few things on it. I didn't like how he did it and tried to show him how to do it my way, the better way. He laughed and asked, "Why do you care how I arrange things?" That reasonable question floored me. I stumbled into the living room and sank into the couch. Why *did* I care how he decorated his own bookshelf? Stunned, I realized he did not appreciate me, never mind worship me. Another night not long after, while he showered, I went looking for answers in the diary I knew he kept under his side of the bed. I read an entry that explored his recent experience of performing. It said nothing about how beautiful I looked or how powerfully I sang during that show. Instead, he'd written things I wished I had not read.

    Jealousy flooded me. I spent the night with my pal Fiona, who still lived in the Mission. She told me to ditch Buck. Said he was selfish and that the music didn't satisfy me, either. But it was all I had. I did not have the energy to start over again, find another boyfriend, find another band.

My life sucked. Hungover the next day, on a rare breezeless morning where the sun shone bright and warm, the putrid smell of overripe tomatoes in outdoor bins in front of the produce store on 16th Street and Valencia made me sick and I puked on the sidewalk.

I left Buck, and the band ended without ceremony, like our relationship had.

After that band crapped out, so did my income. On my hostess job alone I could not make ends meet. I had quit my side jobs months ago to make time for the band, and here I was, once again unable to afford my own apartment. But as sad as the loss of privacy would be, I would not miss the view from the picture window: an overgrown lot between apartment buildings where feral cats took turns sitting on a tilted ceramic commode held up by weeds. Nor did I mind saying goodbye to the moldy shower curtain that stuck to my legs when I shampooed the cigarette smoke out of my hair. I'd somehow learn to live without the rough, grayish industrial carpet and dark, narrow hallways where my neighbors and I never made eye contact. I was more than ready to leave behind a slew of sad-sack memories.

I was so tired of this. It was my sixth move in the less than four years since I'd left Brad. Lucky me, I didn't need to look too long. An ad popped up in the back of the *SF Weekly* placed by a young professional woman with a room to rent in her two-bedroom Art Deco apartment on Fell Street near Steiner—yet another corner of my beloved Alamo Square.

Swollen Appetite

Chapter 16 - Box Full of Wires

In my interview with the woman with the room to rent, it startled me how much younger, better educated, thinner, and therefore prettier she was than me. She could have made a go of it in LA. She owned her own car, had a college degree, and worked a professional nine-to-five job. And somehow she also managed to be an innovative and active artist. Her massive paintings covered the walls throughout the flat, and after I moved in, she painted several teensy-weensy ones for the bare walls in my new bedroom. Vassa was from El Paso, but did not have a Texas accent. She was different from anyone else I knew, and I came to understand her quirks as geekiness. She had focus, concentration, and a head for math. Vassa and her friends knew a lot about computers, and even used them at their jobs.

The little bedroom Nellie and I occupied had a window overlooking Fell Street. My view was the backside of Ida B. Wells High School, plus a retaining wall with a broken-glass mosaic of a giant hummingbird feeding on flowers. It sparkled on sunny days. On the hill to the right of the high school sat a majestic Victorian, the Henry Ohlhoff House. Little did I know it housed recovering addicts and alcoholics. Cars rushed up the hill to the traffic light at Steiner, slowed or stopped, and then accelerated down the hill to Divisadero. Whoosh, whoosh. It sounded like the ocean's tide as I blew cigarette smoke from my new window.

In the living room Vassa kept two domestic short-haired cats, an albino boa constrictor with red eyes, and a terrarium of mushroom-colored horned lizards. A gold-framed photo of Vassa's great-aunt nuzzling a Chihuahua sat on the fireplace mantel. The ornately carved, wooden-legged, gold brocade couch was home to three cats now that Nellie had moved in. A massive saltwater aquarium took up most of the real estate on the 1950s-diner-style table in the kitchen. UPS delivered a box of live crickets once a week to feed the lizards. Oftentimes the insects escaped from the cages and hid in the many nooks and crannies of the dark wood wall paneling of our flat built just after the 1906 earthquake. Our apartment sounded like a campsite. At night, on my way down the bare wood floor of the hallway to the one toilet we shared (in a separate room from the shower and sink), I'd step on errant crickets and slide on their guts. Once a month, Vassa brought a live mouse from the pet store to feed the boa constrictor. Oftentimes those mice died of fright before the snake ate them. Then our apartment thrummed with the beating of one less wild heart.

Vassa would sit at a small desk in the corner of the kitchen, plunking away at her computer while I mixed myself a drink. As she explained something technical, I felt the encroaching shift in culture and envisioned myself waiting tables forever. I put the vodka back in the freezer and shoved that scary thought aside—told myself not to worry, that I needn't bother with all that computer stuff because of my strong songwriting skills. I would sell my songs, full of real-life experiences, to someone with a big recording career. I did not have to understand a box full of wires. *I've seen more in my short life than all these young computer nerds put together.* I went back to my room and tried to hush the noise in my head with my vodka and grapefruit.

I forced myself to interact with Vassa's friends when they hung out, always in the kitchen. An old Gen-Xer, still a slacker at thirty-two, I'd grab a beer from the fridge or a quick bite before a work shift and tell the young'uns my most outlandish stories. Sometimes they showed interest, but they went to different bars, knew different bands, and possessed a whole scene of their own. They schemed about where they'd "tag" before the trains stopped running and I felt stupid for asking what tagging meant.

My roommate and I bonded nonetheless over art, our love of cats, and an appreciation for country music. She came to my shows with her sister. They'd lived in Texas and knew how to swing dance, and with the neo-swing revival on the rise, bands like the Squirrel Nut Zippers and Royal Crown Revue, and local acts like the Atomic Cocktails or Lavay Smith and Her Red Hot Skillet Lickers, united the cousin scenes of rockabilly, jump blues, Western swing, and indie alt-country on the dance floors of Blondie's Bar, the Elbo Room, and Bimbo's 365 Club.

Now I could dance to something besides techno at The Stud.

A cylindrical tank of African dwarf frogs sat on the nightstand beside Vassa's bed. The tiny frogs would swim to the surface for a sip of air, then sink in slow motion to the gravel at the bottom. Slowly up, then a slow freefall, one by one. Watching their surges and sinkings soothed my pounding hangover. I'd sit at her bedside in her windowless bedroom, lit only by the aquarium light, after she went to work. I hid my swollen, red face from her in the mornings. A lovely, smart, and wholly decent person, Vassa shouldn't be worrying about me. On those mornings when my hands shook and I might be able to get a piece of toast down, I saw myself in the bathroom mirror above the sink stained blue and purple from Vassa's Manic Panic hair dye. I looked drained, leached, splotchy, bloated. I covered my gray flesh with makeup like a mortician painting a corpse. Unable to draw my eyeliner straight and having forgotten to take my makeup off the night before, I patted paint on top of peeling paint and ran for work.

    I was lost, unmoored, band free, and lover deficient. I craved news that might give me a boost, so I began to visit psychics. Sometimes paying someone to tell me what I wanted to hear worked. My eyes stayed on the sidewalk as I trudged down the hill on Fell Street to Mad Magda's Russian Tea Room in Hayes Valley. My future lurched and groaned with bad brakes instead of bright lights and applause. Seeing younger people on a regular basis at Vassa's apartment made me realize my youth had passed, and that I had squandered it. I sought guidance from the clairvoyant. At the teahouse, a blind Belgian woman read my tarot cards. She was made up in sparkling eyeshadow and lipstick, and her long gray hair was coiffed and studded with ornamental combs. Silk scarves draped over a scarlet-red velvet robe enshrouding her shoulders. Someone loved and tended to her. I craved her regal kindness almost as much as I did whiskey. She did not hide her blind eyes behind sunglasses, and they rolled around willy-nilly as she pulled cards from a deck and laid them down for me to see. Her liver-spotted hand deciphered the braille. The Prince of Cups meant I had returned from being estranged from all I held dear, a homecoming after a long journey. The Ten of Swords alongside it meant something had ended, or was about to end, and a revival was not to be expected.

"What does this mean to you?" she asked.

I scoured the corners of my mind for anything that needed to end or kept me estranged. Didn't my last few relationships with men and my bands fit that description? She frowned: "It's something deeper." My drinking problem I was not ready to admit. Didn't matter that she was blind; she saw me.

Vassa liked psychics, too, and always wanted to hear about my sessions. She also loved self-help books. She loaned me books by Cheri Huber, a Zen Buddhist. Some days, I felt like a wan, see-through version of myself, tired and directionless. Even masturbation had become too much work. I needed a shot in the arm, and so I became willing to read the books, thinking maybe I'd find renewal in them. I did, but it took a while.

As the year 1995 strained toward its end, my life consisted of going to work, then going home and drinking enough in my room to pass out. I hid empty bottles under my twin bed. I woke up plenty in the middle of the night and would chew a Sominex or smoke pot even though I hated it. Anything to help me sleep. I blew cigarette smoke out the window into the dark night and whimpered, desperate for rest.

Then I'd get up again and trudge along Fillmore Street toward Japantown. One morning on my walk to work, the stench of burned plastic mixed with Comet singed my nostrils as I passed beneath a shoddy apartment building. *Oh shit!* I ran and tried to hold my breath the length of the block. No way was I going to ingest crack smoke. That shit was instantly addictive. I ran past the El Bethel Terrace apartments, the El Bethel Barbershop, and the pawnshop where I had hocked my wedding ring four years before. I didn't exhale until I crossed Golden Gate and passed McDonald's, where I inhaled big breaths of the wholesome smell of french fries. In my marrow, I knew if I got anywhere near crack, it would lead me to an ugly, ugly death. Not that alcohol would be any prettier. My face was bloated and splotchy with burst capillaries. But because I now had health insurance, I had gone to the dermatologist and had a gin blossom removed from my nose.

I huffed along Fillmore to the Miyako, past the condemned red-brick church building at the corner of McAllister, past the weird athletic shoe store carrying off-brand sneakers just before Geary. Then I saw it. A bench painted with the question, "Are you sick and tired of being sick and tired?" A Kaiser Permanente ad stopped me in my tracks—not because I could answer that question with a simple yes, but because I myself had written a country ballad called "Tired of Being Tired." I was sure someone in Kaiser's marketing department had either overheard me practicing the song or saw me perform it with one of my bands. *Fuck you, Kaiser! You ripped me off!*

My head hurt and my gut was a queasy knot of eels. I was under a spell, out of control and paranoid. Everything felt like a threat—people stealing my songs, time stealing my beauty, lovers stealing my best years. I argued in my head nonstop. *Fuck you! I don't give a fuck. I choose to tread home in boots without socks. It doesn't matter how I got the fist-size bruise on my right ass cheek. I'm not THAT old. My album will be mercurial, and so what if it languishes in obscurity! This is the price I have to pay to lay the truth on all y'all lame cocksuckers.* No amount of alcohol turned these thoughts off. I sat by my open window, an ashtray overflowing on the nightstand, and drank and smoked and watched traffic. I could not get a buzz, I could not get sleepy. My medicine had turned into snake oil.

I spent more time in my bedroom than out in the living room or kitchen with Vassa and her friends. I called old friends in faraway places and held extensive conversations I couldn't remember a goddamn word of. The long cord attached to my phone was not long enough to reach the bathroom. Tethered, I peed into my potted plants if need be. I squatted over the soil and prattled on and on about some injustice or hassle. On one of these binges, my former sister-in-law said she worried about me being a drunk wreck at six in the evening. She said that

Brad had told her when I first moved to San Francisco that he thought I left him so I could drink more—which she'd staunchly refuted. "Was he right?" she asked now. Then she told me not to call her when I had been drinking. That stung and stuck in my craw. *My former sister-in-law thinks I have a drinking problem.*

On what had become a rare excursion—going out to hear live music—I boarded the 22 Fillmore to the Bottom of the Hill to see Howe Gelb perform solo. His band Giant Sand had been one of my favorite indie-rock groups. The brakes hissed as the driver slowed and the trolley pole click-clicked as it connected and juiced along the overhead electric lines. The bus whined up the hills, then ground to a halt at the end of every block in the lower Haight and through the Mission to Potrero Hill. I bobbed and jerked in my seat, then got off a few blocks away from the nightclub to get a smoke in before the show. I weaved around strewn car-window glass—a thieves' mosaic glittering under the streetlights that lit up the fronts of warehouses, some abandoned, some still in use. I showed my ID at the door and paid admission, then grabbed a Bass ale at the curved bar and headed out back to the patio to smoke. Christmas lights were strung across the patio and Howe Gelb stood tall as a tree under them, talking to whoever stepped up. Girls swarmed him, and I inched closer and tried to act nonchalant. He laughed and admitted that his daughter was crazy about Barney, the purple dinosaur from the popular TV show. Someone scoffed, "Ewwww, Barney!" Trying to score points, I jumped to defend Howe's little girl's taste in celebrity dinosaurs. During the show, I got blasted, drunker than shit, and wrote a messy poem in the blank margins of the venue's monthly show calendar. I presented it to Mr. Gelb after the show. He signed it and handed it back to me: "Keep on waxing. Love, Howe."

I wanted more.

As the crowd thinned out and I wobbled at the bar, Ramona, the bar owner and bartender that night, told me to go sit my wasted ass on the curb outside and wait for the cab she'd called me. "Go home," she admonished.

It wasn't the first time that tough, beautiful broad took care of me—or, I reckon, a thousand other drunks.

Consumption

Here comes the cab

The headlights expose warehouse desire

I stumble at the curb

A blanket of booze that warmed me from the inside out

Is tangled around my feet

Grace is not my best feature—I have too many teeth

Wanting to tear into a jugular that spews beauty

Beauty is terror (damn straight)

I want him in my bed

I seek what he does

I am a two-headed barracuda constantly consuming

I stopped going out. My stomach hurt not only from alcohol destroying its lining, but from anxiety. The drinks I could keep down were beer or white wine. It had been a good long while since I could count on a reliable buzz. Some nights just a few drinks made me loopy, but then there were times when I could drink until dawn and still not pass out. No longer did I have a saucy story I couldn't wait to tell Fiona. Or gossip with Billy and Mia that left me feeling superior to the subject matter. I had nothing to say. More often than not, I drank in my room after work, a pack of cigarettes sucked down to the nubs. A dead fly dangled from a sooty, abandoned spiderweb in the corner of my window sash. *How long had it been hanging there?* I knew I was that fly: just another uneaten, unwanted, wasted life.

Thank goodness for Vassa and those books she loaned me. I sat on my twin bed, an ashtray on the windowsill, and smoked and read. One in particular, *The Fear Book* by Cheri Huber, pulled the wool from my eyes. It told me to put the book down and close my eyes and let fear flood my body. What did the scared voices tell me?

> *You blew it.*
> *You aren't as talented as you think.*
> *You've lost your looks.*
> *You're not even second-rate at this point.*
> *There's nowhere to go to start over.*
> *You are killing yourself with alcohol.*

I did not want to die and I did not want to start over. I was stuck. I thought Buddhism would provide some much-needed peace, but instead, it started a fire. My defenses went up in smoke. All of a sudden I could not unsee my alcoholism. Vassa also brought me a book from the checkout aisle at Safeway that explained how the bodies of some people process alcohol differently than others, and that certain foods help clean toxins from overtaxed livers. Help was on the way.

Chapter 17 - Not My Last Drink

I stopped writing songs during those empty hours between meal rushes at the Miyako hostess stand, but I did push-ups and leg lifts in the hallway when no one was around. Even demoralized, I needed to stay in shape. I tried to be discreet as I looked at the want ads in the *Chronicle*. I kept it folded in easy-to-hide squares under a seating chart and later pored over it, looking for additional work. I would do anything not to be alone with my thoughts.

Mecca, a swanky new supper club set to open on Market Street in the Castro, advertised various job openings. I applied for a food server position, got hired on the opening dinner crew, and trained for six weeks with the chef, notable winemakers, cheesemakers, and reps from up-and-coming local ranches and farms. I worked breakfast and lunch shifts at the Miyako hotel restaurant, and waited tables several nights a week at Mecca. Thrilled to be caught up in the prestigious swirl and media blitz that followed its opening, I crushed hard on my manager, which made showing up for work exciting. She flirted right back but had better judgment about me than I had about myself. A power vacuum, I continued to attach myself to anyone I perceived as important. The money was good and the crew liked to party. My fellow waiters and I sometimes got off work in time to catch a band at Cafe du Nord, but most nights we went to Lucky 13. If the wait for the pool table was long, we'd put our names on the board at the Expansion. Or Fiona and I headed over to the newest and coolest bar in the Mission, the Make Out Room, where we tucked into a booth and got lost in the lap steel of the Old Joe Clarks or Paula from Tarnation's unearthly soprano.

I inherited a short-scale white Fender bass and a small practice amp Fiona bought from Black Market Music on 3rd Street in SoMa. She said I'd use it before she would and encouraged me to work on music. The sound would cut out thanks to its dirty pots and a short in the back of the amp until I wiggled the sticky black electrical-taped wires just the right way.

My other friend, Mia, had moved in with a guy I had dated a few years earlier, the drummer from Western Electric. We were all very adult about it. In fact, Mia asked me to house-sit and feed their cats while they were out of town for a long weekend. That sounded like a nice change of scenery—a weekend way out on Taraval and 19th Avenue. I took the bass and amp over ahead of time because I hoped to learn to play while they were gone, without witnesses. Excited, I unearthed a stash of herbal ecstasy I'd been saving for a special occasion. Learning to play bass seemed very special indeed.

After work, I got a little too loaded at a bar I didn't know somewhere between Japantown and the Panhandle. Since I knew a shortcut through that part of Golden Gate

Park—I had explored it on the epic walks of my unemployed days—I headed into the park drunk and cocky. When I came to, out of a blackout, night had fallen in thick, black, felt-tip swipes. I was terrified, lost in the night woods. Unable to see squat, I thrashed around for an eternity until I heard traffic and clawed my way toward it. I burst through the underbrush onto Park Presidio, and nearby Lincoln Way beckoned. That led to Taraval and my friends' house.

The first cab that appeared stopped for me and I gave the driver the address on Taraval, but when we got there, I realized I was out of cash. I must have spent it all at the bar. In the past, cab drivers had always found my shenanigans much cuter than this guy had. He did agree, however, to take me back to my place on Fell Street so I could get my hands on more money. I snuck into the apartment, careful not to wake Vassa, but couldn't find any cash. I grabbed a coffee can full of change and headed back outside. The cab driver wanted to throttle me. I do not know what happened after that, but somehow, I ended up back at the Taraval apartment, where my blessed bass and amp waited for me.

Ready to rock, I opened a beer and eased the herbal ecstasy out of its little plastic sleeve. I popped it into my mouth with a ceremonious swig of beer, followed by a much-needed cigarette. I checked on the cats sleeping in their parents' bed, then set up my amp, tried to tune the bass, and hoped for the best. I'd been told to listen to NRBQ and The Meters, because those were some of the finest bass lines ever recorded. It seemed possible I could learn a thing or two throughout the long weekend ahead.

I pushed play on the cassette deck and got frustrated right away. I had to keep rewinding the last ten seconds of the song so I could try again to emulate what I heard. Lots of notes were happening super-fast and I could not keep up. I did not know my way around the frets in the first place, and by the time I found a note that sounded right, the song had moved well past it. Plus the Fender weighed a lot. It hurt my neck and shoulders. Something wasn't right with my heart. It banged in my chest. Plus the karaoke bar behind the apartment building was going at it full-tilt-boogie and I didn't like how they sang. Something very, very wrong was happening to my heart. It now thudded not only in my chest but into my throat. At this point, I had finished all the beers in the fridge and the half bottle of red wine Mia had left on the counter. I had to slow this shit down. Herbal ecstasy was going to give me a goddamn heart attack.

Afraid for my life, I called the suicide hotline/emergency number on the back of my Kaiser card. I'm not sure why I called them instead of 911. When asked if I had been drinking, I said, yes, I'd had two beers. The operator asked if I was a threat to myself or others and I said no. "No, I'm not suicidal but maybe depressed." Even though I might be having a heart attack, I was incapable of asking for the help I needed, I could not admit herbal ecstasy might be killing me. The operator scheduled an appointment for therapy in two weeks.

The sun came up. My hands shook. I had not slept. I pulled the soft middle from a piece of bread and tried to get it into my mouth. My mouth could not make spit because of all the speed in the X. I walked a block to

Safeway and chain-smoked in front of the glass doors while I waited for the store to open. At the stroke of eight, I bought a six-pack of beer and hurried back to the apartment. I drank one after the next until the six were gone and I could nap before work.

The next two weeks were unlike any before. Life moved in slow motion, like walking underwater. I fluttered and made vague sounds at odd intervals. *Huh? What?* I swayed in a state of suspension. There was a therapy appointment on the books, and I trudged toward it. In those two weeks I did not drink much. After seventeen years of a headlong rush to my next drink, I rolled almost to a stop. I still drank some, since I didn't know what else to do with my hands. I walked into the kitchen out of habit, opened a beer, spoke to Vassa, or took it back to my room. The beer did not bring relief. I drank another beer just to be sure, but it didn't do much either.

Kaiser's San Francisco psychiatry complex was in the Richmond District, and my appointment was for 3 pm, July 21, 1996. I took the Geary bus most of the way there but got off early so I could wander around Little Russia, drifting along the street in front of the Chinese restaurants and beneath the gold-painted onion domes of the Orthodox churches. Aromatic eucalyptus groves on the hillsides to the north filled my lungs. In a clean-smelling, dreamlike state I floated into what happened next.

I signed in for my appointment. I had nothing prepared to talk about, but I showed up on time. I stepped across the threshold of the therapist's doorway, and once inside that tiny office, tearful words gushed out of me for the next forty-nine to fifty minutes, primarily about my problems with my mother. The petite, Gap-wearing therapist looked stricken. At the last minute of the session, I blurted out, "I might be an alcoholic." The relieved-looking therapist handed me a card for Kaiser's Chemical Dependency Recovery Program (CDRP) and suggested I make an appointment with them.

Admitting I might be an alcoholic, out loud, to a professional, felt like a gong inside my head had been hit with a fuzzy mallet. I vibrated at a low-decibel frequency on the bus ride home. After I returned to my apartment, I picked up the telephone receiver and called the number on the card even though it was after five o'clock. Technically, I was doing what I was told to do, but it felt good not to have to speak to anyone else about this so-called drinking problem. I left a message and strolled to the kitchen. The phone rang before I was halfway down the hall and I ran back to my room. An after-hours operator from CDRP was on the line, ready to schedule an early morning appointment for me the very next day.

The next morning, I called in sick to work and went for an evaluation in a nondescript building on the corner of Fillmore and Turk. I'd been passing it for years—it was a few blocks away from every apartment I'd had in San Francisco and my current job at the Miyako Hotel.

"Was I having suicidal thoughts?" one of two counselors in my intake asked. "No, I'm just depressed," I replied. The serious and worried-looking other counselor laid the truth on me: alcohol abuse made people depressed. When asked about my family history of alcoholism, I trotted out old Grandpa and for good measure told them my father had been diagnosed with schizophrenia in his early twenties. I wanted them to understand I came by my diagnosis because of someone else's diagnosis and that I had fucked-up genes. The worried-looking counselor said many people from my father's generation had been misdiagnosed, and that it was likely he'd had manic depression. The other counselor asked if I went on spending sprees or had delusions of grandeur. I laughed and said, "Of course, I'm from the South and I am an Aries." That counselor smiled, but the worried one told me I needed to be more serious about my situation. We all agreed I'd probably do well in an outpatient program.

Chapter 18 - When the Universe Gives You Cake, Eat It

I embarked on six weeks of daily outpatient classes at CDRP. Each day began with an eight o'clock group therapy session followed by classes from nine to noon about the medical effects of alcoholism and chemical dependency. I told the woman in human resources at the Miyako why I needed to alter my schedule, and she accommodated me without hesitation. Mecca also treated me well and said I could return whenever I felt ready. The folks at my jobs seemed happy for me—not the least bit judgmental and even less surprised.

In rehab class, we watched slideshows of grossly enlarged alcoholic hearts, dark purple and fatty yellow cirrhosis of the liver, swollen and oozing legs and elephant-shaped feet from gout, and videos of people with alcoholic dementia known as wet brain. We were taught that alcoholism and drug addiction were chronic and progressive conditions that only abstinence could arrest. Alcoholics have obsessive brains, they're like a dog with a bone. Once a thought starts up—say, the idea of drinking—

the brain cannot stop chewing on that idea, especially if it gets a drink. Once a person drinks, those chemicals satisfy hungry, hungry neurons, which physically reinforces the obsession for more. An even deeper ditch gets dug into one's head. Being given the language to understand what had haunted me from childhood, to be able to articulate that I had a thinking problem that led to my drinking problem, really, truly helped. I was told that without exception, alcoholics cannot ever, not in a million years, drink like a normal person. *As if I ever wanted to drink like a normal person!*

    I vacillated between crying bouts and wanting to shout the amazing news from the rooftop. When the loss staggered me, I felt gangly with unhinged terror. The best way I knew how to keep that persistent pack of demons at bay was by getting them drunk and stupid. Now I was being told that my favorite line of defense doesn't work. And until I learned new ways to calm the fuck down, these one-day-at-a-time days felt like whole seasons. I grieved the San Francisco skyline and its lost charms each sober night. I walked at a clip, past bars with open doors, afraid the smell of booze and cigarettes wafting from inside would grip me like the smell of blood to a shark. I did not want to wake up my inner shark. Rehab advised us to get phone numbers from each other and to call one another when the cravings hit, because they would, and we needed to tell on ourselves and be honest about it. To be available to another suffering alcoholic was paramount because only we understood how bad this felt.

    Some days I radiated hope. My body appreciated that the plug had been put back in the jug. I accepted that once a pickle, a cucumber can never be a cucumber again. No more hangovers, no more rotgut, no more bloated face and shaking hands in the morning helped my willingness to not drink. In just a few days my body felt better. Light as a feather and as chirpy as a bird trill, I answered the phone in the afternoons at work. And I took calls from my rehab buddies when they wanted to talk about their cravings. But I hadn't reached out to them first. Not yet. I figured I could handle my cravings on my own.

    Once a week I met with the drug and alcohol counselor overseeing my case. Australian and a former Jesuit priest, he practiced his recovery program in Overeaters Anonymous. He wore his fluffy white hair shoulder length and always sported cowboy boots. He had a congenital hand deformity known as flipper hands: his fingers were webbed together except for his thumb. With a kind heart and gentle spirit he suffered through my bitchin' and moanin' about this and that for six long weeks and didn't take it personally. He also didn't indulge me or give me false hope. One day in his office I complained about the dated, weird, and misogynistic language in the literature I had to read as a recovering alcoholic. He said, well, maybe one day you can write your own recovery book, but for now, look for what resonates. Take what you like and leave the rest. This book has helped millions, he added. Then my counselor listened to a new recording of one of my original country songs from his cassette deck and tapped his boot to the music.

    Another day I complained that my job bored me to distraction and underutilized my intellect. I did next to nothing to earn my paycheck and shouldn't I look for a job that leveraged my big brain. He reminded me that my current job provided insurance and this excellent chemical dependency recovery program and how unwise it would be to push myself now, to engage in unnecessary stress, for at least the first year of my sobriety.

"When the universe gives you cake, eat it," he said.

The group therapy sessions blew my mind. Turns out, anyone could have an alcohol problem. It didn't matter how young or old you were, or which socioeconomic or ethnic background you came from. A woman in her nineties whose husband had just died, as well as teenagers, lawyers, bus drivers, firefighters, teachers, and other restaurant and hotel workers attended the same group therapy sessions that I did. We had nothing and everything in common. Hearing others articulate how I felt but couldn't yet put into words kept me in awe. What could have been my very own story came out of their mouths. One man fantasized about being in Barry Manilow's band when he drank. He hid in the coat closet of his house, away from his wife and kids, with a bottle of gin in his hand and Walkman headphones over his ears, singing late into the night. I had several versions of that fantasy. A teenage girl who shot heroin aspired to pay her mother's rent with the money she made modeling. I had a version of that fantasy as well. Long-held secrets that previously bound me into anxious knots began to loosen. I learned to tell the truth even when it scared me, like to admit I still wanted to buy gallons of whiskey, hole up in a hotel far, far away, and drink myself to death. Others in my group did too. My fears and self-destructive desires were like squid ink; the group was the ocean that could absorb it. At the end of each session when I'd just said the shit that packed my brain out loud, I felt better. Better enough to commit to not drinking the rest of that day and night and to return the next morning to tell the truth.

To feel the side of my face and neck sink into a soft, clean pillow when I went to bed at night became my new favorite activity. I thanked whatever was keeping me sober for not having to drink that day and happily fell into the granny arms of slumber. I had not felt myself drift off to sleep in seventeen long years, more than half of my life. In the morning when I woke up without a hangover, I thought, *How can this be?*

I caught myself skipping along Steiner Street on my way to group therapy and did not stop. Thirty-three and skipping alongside Alamo Square. Not stoned. Not being chased. Just happy to be alive on a sidewalk that seemed plenty wide and not too poopy. I laughed aloud and skipped with purpose. I lost ten pounds without trying. I switched from Marlboro Reds to Marlboro Lights. My spirit soared like a fishing line cast across an inexhaustible blue sky, gleaming in the sun, whistling. At least during the day. The hours after dinner and before going to bed, my old habitual drinking time, haunted me. But Vassa and Fiona had my back. My roommate watched movies with me on the nights I didn't work, and Fiona brought a giant bouquet to me at work at Mecca and took me out to eat. For almost a month I replaced the glasses of wine before bed with goblets of Welch's grape juice and looked at the Henry Ohlhoff House on the corner.

Then Vassa went to visit her mother in Alabama. Standing outside of the heavy wooden apartment door, she warned, "Now don't you go drinking while I'm gone." I assured her it was the last thing on my mind.

That evening on my way home from work, I stopped at the video store on Haight Street near Fillmore and picked up Sean Penn's directorial debut, *The Crossing Guard*, which featured two of my favorite actors, Jack Nicholson and Anjelica Huston. Then I picked up takeout from the health food store next door. At the very last second, before the cashier finished ringing me up, I grabbed a bottle of room-temperature chardonnay from a nearby display case. *One last dance for old times' sake*, I reasoned.

The Crossing Guard joined the long list of 1990s films I got too drunk to finish. After I emptied the chardonnay, I rooted around in the kitchen cabinets until I found a bottle of Seagram's 7 I'm pretty sure Vassa had tried to hide from me, since it was tucked behind some pots and pans in the lowest kitchen cabinet. The gold-plastic screw cap had broken off in a V-shape on one side and almost stayed sealed. I gulped a big chug straight from the bottle. Then I poured water in to get the level back to where I thought it had been and put it back behind the pots and pans. Then I took it back out and poured most of it into a tumbler.

The next morning that empty bottle glared at me from the kitchen counter when I was making coffee. An indictment. And I missed my thirty-day sobriety check-in session with my Australian counselor because I overslept. I called the CDRP office to apologize for missing my appointment and said "I guess that's that," but before I could hang up they put my counselor on the line. He said not to worry, tomorrow is a perfectly fine day to review what happened. The next day was August 22, 1996, and I haven't had a drink since.

I'm an alcoholic.

    I'm an alcoholic.

    Holy shit, I'm an alcoholic!

    I just couldn't get over it. Can you believe it? I'm an alcoholic. I could be brushing my teeth and all of a sudden I'd remember, oh my fucking god, I'm an alcoholic. Or I might be seating a nice couple at a table at YoYo Bistro and, while pulling out the chair for the lady, I'd think, oh jeez—I'm an alcoholic! I told everyone about getting sober. All my friends, family, coworkers, bosses, ex-boyfriends, corner-store owners, everyone, because I did not feel ashamed. More than relieved, I was thrilled. I had the choice to survive a life-threatening illness. Drinking had been hard work, serious business, sometimes exciting for a minute, but not after it occupied my every thought: *When is my next drink? How will I pay for it?* After I began drinking, *Would I black out and lose control?* To not be hungover, and to not worry about what I might have said and done the night before in a blackout, was a deliverance. I started to understand what grace is. What a paradox for a person who lived to drink because I loved it so much, and relied upon it utterly! This person, me, fer chrissake, I am an ALCOHOLIC!

Our outpatient group therapist encouraged us to attend recovery meetings outside of Kaiser because our insurance-supported recovery only lasted so long. That's how people stayed sober for the long haul. But I liked my familiar, clean, not-religious group sessions at Kaiser. I didn't want to go to those anonymous meetings that might be a cult, full of whack jobs. But I was desperate to keep feeling better, which to my surprise kept happening as long as I didn't drink.

The very first non-Kaiser meeting I attended was in the Castro, where I felt safest, near Mecca, where I still worked a few reservation-taking shifts in the quiet and calm afternoons; I'd given up the fast pace of nightly food service and all the temptations serving alcohol brought. Most of the people populating that first twelve-step meeting were gay men. A room of thirty or so men, and two or three women besides myself, passed around a blue book that held personal accounts about the way alcohol had ravaged the life of the storyteller. Each person read one paragraph aloud before handing the book to the person seated next to them. Some of these guys read with flair and were as dramatic as actors. And yet they did not mock what they read even though people laughed. I thought it was weird to laugh about alcoholism.

I sat at the edge of this stark room with worn linoleum, close to the door. I summoned just enough courage to raise my hand when asked if anyone was new to the meeting. I said, "Hi, I'm Sandra, and I'm an alcoholic." And not a peep more. No longer with my chummy little Kaiser group, I felt naked and stupid and ready to run. I slipped out as soon as the hands on either side dropped mine after the meeting ended with the Serenity Prayer. I ran across the trolley tracks and brick island on both sides of stinky old Market Street and headed up Church Street toward Fell.

A woman ran after me. "I want to welcome you and tell you that it gets better. Keep coming back," she said. She handed me her business card and told me to call when cravings hit. She said she had had terrible cravings for a few months after she quit drinking. She smiled and walked away and didn't try to put the moves on me. Weird but nice. I tried a few more meetings at a few more locations. It got easier to speak up.

My French friend Chloe and I had stayed close, and she invited me over to the new flat she had bought on Fulton Street, just across from Alamo Square and a block away from the apartment where she and Tom Rhodes had let me stay when I first moved to town. That romantic partnership was now ancient history. A friend of hers offered to detox me since she needed to accumulate hours for her acupuncture license. The massage table was set up in the living room, facing out at a view of massive redwoods towering on the ridge of the park. Because Chloe and Tom were still on good terms, his Comedy Central special *Viva Vietnam: A White Trash Adventure* played on her tiny television in the background, and we laughed with Tom for old times' sake. Acupuncture needles were stuck into my ears, and Chloe's pal cupped my shoulder blades and upper back with a hot glass that sucked up the skin and muscles, leaving circular bruises the size of sugar cookies that lasted for weeks. I was pretty happy during these young days of sobriety, even though occasional waves of anxiety rolled in. Even so, my neck muscles were knotted and cabled. The woman worked on the knots with muscular hands and lit incense that smelled like burning mud. As she worked on my neck she said, "Just because you've gotten sober doesn't mean bad things won't happen to you."

That comment stung worse than the needles. It undid the good from the acupuncture and pricked my pink cloud.

Then on my last day of daily group therapy at Kaiser, my favorite facilitator told us he'd been diagnosed with liver cancer. Even though he had been clean and sober for well over a decade, the former abuse had taken a toll on his body. My jaw tensed and my stomach hurt. The pretty pink cloud that had buoyed me up so very, very high hissed and plummeted. As the counselor wished us well, his parting words were, "Now's the time to shit or get off the pot." In other words: if we wanted to stay sober, we had to commit to the daily rigors it required. It was time to get a sponsor to continue recovery work in the real world.

Gossip flew around the break room at CDRP that several sober celebrities attended a meeting in the Marina whenever they were in town. The Marina was not a neighborhood I'd spent much time in, but the possibility of seeing my favorite singer in the whole wide world drew me down the steep descent on Fillmore Street. At this rambling old building where meetings took place on the hour every hour into the night, its lobby furnished with donated couches, literature, coffee, and snacks, I found a new place to go. It was like a bar, except we talked about drinking instead of drinking. We smoked outside and took turns cleaning out the big metal cans full of sand and cigarette butts. Standoffish and somewhat mistrustful, I thought I was better than most of the other recovering alcoholics I saw there, but I also needed relief that I could no longer get from a bottle.

> Dear Sushi,
> Will I be able to eat you without sake?

> Dear Sex,
> It's just you and me for a while, okay?

> Dear Moon,
> I drank you dry.

> Dear Alcohol,
> I will miss you forever.

Chapter 19 - Pick Up Your Bed and Walk

I heard the expression that if you hang out at a barbershop, you'll get a haircut. I stayed away from bars and tried to gather sparks. My soul shivered. I needed to rekindle the fire within me without using booze as lighter fluid, so I took myself to church one Sunday morning. In the size 4 black Bebe jacket I had taken from the lost and found at Mecca, I stood outside Glide Memorial Church with a cast of San Francisco characters waiting for the eleven o'clock service. I felt squirrelly, but I looked sharp. The earlier service was packed full of devout, regular members, but the line for this celebration was filled with European tourists, alternative thinkers, and late sleepers. A good portion of us smoked. Homeless people walked up and down the line asking for money and cigarettes. Glide fed, housed, educated, and helped those who asked for help. I might have taken more than I gave, but at least now I could share my Marlboros.

Fiona—still my best friend—and I had been going to Glide every so often for a while, mainly for the music. We weren't religious, but Glide didn't preach religion. It was, and is, a spiritual experience, proud of its diverse community, a magnet for regular people of all colors, glorious gays, guppies, artists, poor folks, politicians, and celebrities, like Sharon Stone, whom I saw several times when she was married to a prominent San Francisco businessman, rubbing shoulders with hat-wearing ladies of the Glide community. Ashford & Simpson sometimes sang with the choir, and Maya Angelou always got up and spoke when she was in town. Everyone was welcome, and it made going to church exciting.

Glide gave a much-needed boost to my anemic spirit. It seemed as San Francisco as the Golden Gate Bridge. Steeped in social justice and spiritual inclusiveness, Cecil Williams delivered the message, and the Glide Ensemble and the Glide Change Band, led by John Turk, delivered the music. Glide wove healing sutures into my reckless and bloody heart every single time I availed myself. I went just often enough to become familiar with the soloists, like Carolyn Huggins, who sang "God Is Good to Me" from her wheelchair at the front of the stage. Fiona and I couldn't wait for Cecil to hand the mic to the gorgeous Ms. Emma Jean Foster (whom we called Whitney Houston). And after that tear-fest, Roosevelt Winchester brought us to our feet and had us clapping hands and singing along as we danced in our pews to "Restore My Joy."

This Sunday, I went by myself. The church was already overflowing, so I stood in the back. I was headed to work right after the service and leaving from there would be faster than removing myself from the middle of a packed pew. I was still accustomed to looking for a back door, preferring an easier way out. This getting-sober business was hard. My rose-colored-glasses-wearing denial liked to point out that drinking made life more palatable. My last drink had been recent enough for me to know that wasn't true.

I was hovering around ninety days sober, and physically, I felt so much better. But my thinking was far from fixed. Kaiser's chemical dependency classes taught us that if you didn't have a plan to stay sober, you might have an unconscious plan to drink. I wasn't a regular anywhere. Not at Glide, and not at any specific recovery meeting. I wasn't all in. If I was serious about this sober thing, I needed to ask someone in recovery to show me how she stayed sober. I needed a guide, a sponsor. Not ready to look just yet, though, I didn't know if I wanted anyone to tell me what to do.

The music that day soared. And the crowd celebrated. Glide had set me on my feet emotionally in the past, but maybe because I was there by myself, and standing in the back, I wasn't feeling it. I was not as connected and uplifted as I wanted to be. But as soon as Reverend Cecil Williams started his sermon, I perked right up. Oftentimes he wore a tailored suit or a dashiki. On this day, a purple robe flowed around his every gentle move. And he moved a lot, constantly, between the congregation and the ensemble. A stack of Post-it notes sat on the good Reverend's podium, and on each one he had written a Bible verse on the top half and an interpretation on the bottom half—what he thought it meant today, in real time, for real people. He picked up a Post-it, read the message, then gave it to someone nearby. As the pale-yellow stack diminished, the ensemble stood back up and began to sing softly, swaying, building in intensity for Williams's final delivery. John Turk delivered well-timed organ fills. Williams made his way more than halfway down the center aisle through the congregation, speaking into his cordless mic, reading the Bible passage and interpretation, and then entrusted it to a parishioner. He swirled around and headed back toward the pulpit, presumably having completed the passages. As he neared the choir, they sang more full-throated, and the rest of the band joined in.

Then, with a deliberate flourish, the Reverend swung back around and announced, "I have one more passage!" He walked back down the aisle, robe flowing, smile as bright and beautiful as God ever made, and headed toward the very back of the church, the cheap seats where the restless-hearted stirred. That dear man did not know me, but he made a good assessment. Our eyes locked for what seemed like ten minutes as he closed the distance. When he reached me, I got to see what unconditional love looks like.

The Reverend raised his cordless mic and read from the last Post-it: "Jesus said, 'Pick up your bed and walk.' What that means to me is: NOW is the time for recovery!" Cecil handed me the Post-it and I sobbed on his shoulder.

Don't get me wrong. I didn't go to church for Jesus. Jesus and I broke up when I was in middle school. A resurrection of that relationship wasn't what happened at Glide Memorial that Sunday morning. Encouraged and solidified, not rendered a sorrowful sinner, I had received a cosmic nudge in front of hundreds of people to commit to sobriety and I would, goddammit!

I scotch-taped that Post-it above the light switch in my bedroom on Fell Street. Every time I flipped the switch, I remembered that there is love. Big, velvety, juicy love, like what I saw in the Reverend's eyes, and I wanted that more than I wanted a drink. I hurried to recovery meetings and searched for someone to help me with sobriety, someone with the emotional fortitude I wanted for myself. I knew I'd found my sponsor when I heard a woman talk about how depressed she had been, how she had broken her own heart. She said she didn't get sober to become a "good girl." She got sober to become sane. This woman possessed grit and depth, and the courage to be herself even when she felt lousy. I feared how I felt and did not know how to articulate it. Over cigarettes outside on the sidewalk, I asked her to be my sponsor.

On a cold, foggy sidewalk in the Marina, that woman said, "Yes."

Chapter 20 - God-Given Talent

Having a sponsor meant I could learn to ask for help. Strong willed and self-reliant since childhood, recovery asked me to take a look at why I was like that and how it did not serve me anymore. Unaware of the benefits of not having to know everything, it took a while to get in the habit.

The cravings for alcohol gave me impetus to call my sponsor. "How the fuck is it that a few months ago I couldn't *not* drink, then yesterday was fine, I didn't think about it once, but today is awful, I'm going crazy—I can't stop thinking about drinking!"

When I admitted to my new sponsor that I wanted to drink (instead of just hoping the cravings would go away), she stayed on the phone with me until the cravings passed.

I liked her lots, which helped. I appreciated being understood. As we dug into our recovery thing, I asked for more insights.

"Do you think I should keep writing songs and singing?"

"Hell yeah, you should."

"You don't think it's a waste of time?"

"It doesn't matter what I think. Your talent is God given."

At her encouragement, I decided to invest in my music career by taking singing lessons. I took a cassette of Western Electric's demo songs and played our version of George Jones and Tammy Wynette's "Something to Brag About" for my new teacher. It was my first lesson and I wanted to make a good impression, give him a good idea of what he had to work with. After listening to less than thirty seconds of the song, he clicked off the cassette player and announced that Tammy Wynette was not a singer worth emulating. The urge to walk out the door hit me hard. Instead, I held back tears and took the sheet music he handed me for several Broadway show tunes, but told him I didn't know how to read sheet music. From the piano he said to try following along anyway, which I did for the next goddamn hour. That Wynette comment festered. When I went to the second lesson, anger sat close to the surface, and I feared I might yell "eat shit" and leave. But we managed to plow under yet another hour of my life without an outburst on my part.

Frustrated, I called my sponsor. I worried over the phone that by not liking Tammy Wynette, he didn't like me. Plus, my future lies in country music, not show tunes! I trusted my sponsor with my tangled-up thoughts, not because she was an authority but because she had lots of tangled-up thoughts, too. She reminded me that I had choices. I did not have to stick with this guy who didn't get me. She noted how I'd stuck with old boyfriends who didn't get me, and that I could do things differently. Relieved, I canceled further appointments with the voice teacher without feeling the need to tell him how much he sucked.

I called my sponsor when my schedule at work changed without anyone consulting me. She asked me how that made me feel. That question stumped me. "Mad?" I supposed. "Mad enough to drink?" "No, just pissed off." She asked a few more questions and, with her help, I discovered I felt all kinds of things, including hurt, overlooked, underappreciated, and trapped. I found out that my go-to emotion was anger but that in truth, I was a sensitive woman with a tapestry of feelings just below that anger. She reminded me that I had little experience navigating strong emotions without becoming overwhelmed, and that in the past, I had rushed to change those feelings, usually with a cocktail. So, my sponsor helped me reason things out. She asked me if I would miss something important by complying with the new schedule. "Not really," I replied. Then she suggested I focus on the good aspects of my job rather than the unpleasant ones and to call her again, anytime, especially if I wanted to drink. She gave practical suggestions her sponsor had given her, stuff I could remember, like that being uncomfortable never killed anyone but drinking did. And to get my ass to a meeting and talk about it more.

"Lots of people feel the way you do," she said. "Share it. Tell them you called your sponsor and she told you to talk about it at a meeting."

So strange how this simple, unoriginal suggestion worked.

Not long after I started working with my recovery sponsor, my Miyako supervisor scheduled me to take a liquor inventory of the hotel bar between breakfast and lunch shifts—when absolutely no one else would be there and not a soul would see if I happened to take a nip. I counted the twinkling, beautiful, shapely, jewellike bottles lining the shelves: blue Sapphire, amber Jack, icy-aqua Patrón, electric-green Chartreuse. What a monumental departure for me to behold their majesty without sneaking a snort! Hollow-legged and faint-hearted, I would need grace and courage to handle this particular work task and not fall off the wagon.

I radiated "help," the most humble and practical prayer I knew, as I sweated and wiped down a partially full bottle of Ketel One. Ketel One is delicious. Even though I wanted a taste, I simply recorded its ounces on my clipboard. As I held that already-open bottle in my hands I felt really, really sad. I missed vodka so damn much. Muzak and self-pity washed over me. Yet I pushed forward with my task. I tallied and wiped and measured and when I finished the inventory, I called my sponsor. Only another alcoholic could understand how hard that experience had been. And see the victory in getting through it without drinking.

For months now, I had woken up bright-eyed and bushy-tailed, bouncing off the walls. I didn't know what to do with all that energy and time. It piled up like staticky blankets, and blue sparks flew between my idle hands. The drinking life takes up a lot of time. At a conservative estimate, I drank five hours a day every day for seventeen years. That equals 31,025 hours of my life. But how does a person calculate the real costs—all the time spent nursing hangovers or ruminating on regrettable behavior or chasing down loved ones or bosses with apologies or looking for new jobs? Now, recovery meetings used up one hour a day.

    I needed healthy new ways to occupy myself. I switched gears from voice lessons to learning to play the bass that Fiona had given me. In the *SF Weekly* I found a person named Tyrone advertising bass lessons. Fender strapped to my back, I lugged my gear past the Mexican modernist mural above the café at the corner of sweeping Dolores Park to the crest of the hill and my teacher's building. Tyrone was a super-enthusiastic young rocker dude with a shaved head. He lived and taught in a tiny room under a staircase that the two of us could squeeze together in, but not play our basses at the same time. Tyrone clearly needed the money, and expressed as much awe in me staying sober as in my learning to play an instrument so late in life. He revered Bowie almost as much as I did, and didn't judge my country music inclinations.

    Tyrone showed me how to play my own songs and the covers I wanted to learn. He told me to practice my scales without looking at my hands, and to practice often, without amplification, while I watched TV or spoke on the phone. "You can't get better if you don't play. Therefore, practice, practice, practice."

    The desire to play an instrument filled me with purpose. Maybe now I could play my songs the way I heard them in my head. At home, I sang with joy and came up with bass lines for new songs. I sat on the side of my twin bed and hammered out the major and minor scales, thickening the pads on my fingertips. I did not use a pick because I liked the feel of the heavy-gauge strings, like dragging my fingers across a chain-link fence.

The first songs I learned were simple, like George Jones's "Waltz of the Angels" and the Bottle Rockets' "Queen of the World," as well as the songs I had written and all the new songs I was writing. I started playing bass because, first, I already had a bass thanks to Fiona, and, second, there were scads of guitarists in the world, but not enough bass players. Beyond pragmatism, I ended up loving the bass because it gives every song an ass to shake. Makes 'em move. I had rhythm and good timing and I played and sang for hours in the afternoons in my bedroom, annoying the cat but not my neighbors. They did not have to pound on my walls and tell me to quiet down because now that I wasn't drunk and delirious, I considered how the sounds I made affected them.

At the ripe old age of thirty-three, I was ready to play music with other musicians, sober, with bass lines moving through me like thundershowers in the spring. Thank God for Joe Henry's *Trampoline*, Willie Nelson's *Phases and Stages*, Dead Can Dance, and Emmylou Harris, whose recordings lulled me to sleep each night. I listened for the bass lines in every song, and those rhythms wound through my dreams. I dreamed of Emmylou, dressed in a short white brocade skirt and wearing patent-leather go-go boots. She held my hand and we two-stepped over a bridge above an alligator-infested moat that surrounded a tower that rose through the clouds and cracked open the universe. With my hand in hers, she guided me up the steps of the

Tower of Song. The purest of songbirds led me to my perch.

    Dear Muse,
    We're in love, aren't we.
    PS. Your hair smells like fennel and honey.

Chapter 21 - My Toes Curled in My Boots

Just because I had gotten sober didn't mean I stopped going to psychics. If anything, my interest grew. That big ol' hole, that piece that was missing that I had tried to fill with red wine and bourbon, was still there, but without alcohol gushing into the echoing canyon some people call a God-shaped hole, I had to find new ways to fill it. Like playing the bass and going to meetings and Glide services and writing songs and having my tarot cards read. My sponsor also had a big ol' hole and she enjoyed having her fortune told as well. Together, we augmented our recovery practice by attending talks and seminars by the Inner Light Foundation's leading spiritualist, Betty Bethards.

Bethards gave motivational speeches and guided meditations at that modernized Gothic brownstone church on the corner island between Gough and Geary and O'Farrell, the First Unitarian Universalist Society of San Francisco. If you arrived an hour early, you could get in line to ask her a question. Betty knew things, she was a psychic, and I expected to have an exciting future. The first time I asked her a question, I asked if cultivating my singing talent was what I was meant to do in this life. What I wanted her to say was, "You bet your ass—you're on the path to becoming a rich and famous singer-songwriter." Instead, she said it didn't matter what I did as long as I worked with people. That seemed more like a psychological observation than a psychic one. A shitty fortune cookie. But Betty's talks thrilled me nonetheless because of her theatrical presentation. That old woman kept a nice figure and good hair and a younger boyfriend. She must have had the ear of God.

While the Inner Light Foundation fed into my recovery practice, *The Artist's Way Workbook* fed my artistic development. I decoded my dreams for their deeper spiritual meanings using Betty's bestseller, *The Dream Book*, while writing my morning pages that *The Artist's Way* suggested, all the while practicing the conscious contact with my higher power that my recovery suggested. Another trinity! I sat on my bed each morning with a cup of coffee and a pen and wrote and read and meditated. I filled journal after journal, the lead scientist on my own archaeological dig. I drew a tunnel to the holy spirit with a ballpoint pen.

Around this time I re-met Tonette. I needed change for the 22 Fillmore bus one afternoon after a meeting, when I saw a familiar-looking woman standing on the corner of Fillmore and Union. A few years earlier, Tonette and I had been introduced because she organized the cabaret night where my friend Mia sang. Now, at the bus stop, still as sweet as pie, Tonette gladly changed my five-dollar bill.

Uniquely fashionable, her style had shifted from goth to rockabilly, and she was as stunning as ever with her slow smile, blue-green movie-star eyes, and soft shoulders.

We boarded the 22 and Tonette turned around in the seat in front of me as the bus lumbered around the mansion-lined streets of Pacific Heights. We got to talking about country music and she told me about her boyfriend's band, The Rounders. They were performing a Hank Williams birthday tribute show at the Hi-Ball in North Beach that weekend and she invited me to come. We also decided to get together and sing old-timey country songs. Maybe, she said, her boyfriend's band would have us sing a few songs with them as a duo. What perfect timing! It had been six months since I had last sung in a band. *The Artist's Way* promised that synchronicity would happen if you showed up for it.

Tonette mentioned that she played drums in the garage-rock band the Kirby Grips, and I told her I was learning to play bass. Maybe we could get a little band of our own up and running? Coincidentally, she knew my roommate, Vassa, from responding to each other's ads in the *SF Weekly* for gals looking for swing-dance partners. We exchanged numbers.

That weekend, for the first time since I had stopped drinking, I went to a bar that I did not work in, the Hi-Ball on Broadway. My sponsor went with me for support. We had a good reason to be in a bar: live music. The Rounders provided backing music as various singers stepped up on stage and sang their favorite Hank Williams songs. My sponsor and I watched in sober solidarity. Then the band took a break and we went outside to smoke.

Swollen Appetite

Out on the sidewalk, Tonette introduced me to one of the guitarists in the band, Brian Mello. My sponsor, a hopeless romantic, assessed the situation, ground out her cigarette butt with her heel, made the "call me" sign with her hand to her ear, and said good night. Tonette also peeled away and left the handsome, tall guitarist alone with me. I lunged into talking about music and tattoos. I lamented not being able to decide on anything that would last forever. Brian mentioned he had a few tattoos, but only after I asked. That seemed super cool to me, especially since he had designed them. For such a stylish guy, he was so sweet, and shy. I wasn't used to shy men. Our taste in music collided and we discussed David Bowie, X, and the undervalued Canadian rockers April Wine with passion. Conversation flowed, but then it was time for him to go back on stage. I said goodnight. As cute as he was, I did not want to push my luck in a bar on my own, so I hightailed it home.

A few days later Tonette came over to the Fell Street apartment and we worked up the songs "Crazy Arms" and "Apartment #9" to take to a Rounders rehearsal.

"Tell me everything you know about Brian Mello," I said.

"Well, he lives in San Jose, has played in some crazy-good bands, and is super sweet. But he might have a girlfriend." I frowned and Tonette vowed to find out more.

Crickets chirped in the background of the rehearsal tapes we recorded on my Panasonic boombox in the living room next to Vassa's great horned lizards. I loved singing with Tonette and realized I had not worked on music with a woman before. Even though both of us were dead serious about our musicianship, it felt easy and playful to work together. We decided to call ourselves the Blue Dolls in honor of the Anita Carter tune.

Two weeks later, patches of blue sky peeked out from behind the fog when I threw open the curtains. Sunlight dappled the wood floor, and I realized I did not dread a goddamn thing. I borrowed Vassa's metallic-blue 1960s-vintage leather jacket and wore it to the Rounders rehearsal at Lennon Studios, on Dore Street near the I-80 onramp, where Tonette and I would audition to sing backups. I knew I looked good in Vassa's jacket and felt cooler than shit when Tonette and I sashayed into Room 10.

The bottoms of my boots stuck to the gummy studio carpet. The thickened pile reeked from years of cigarette ash and spilled beer. I felt like I had come home. Tonette introduced me to her boyfriend and bandleader on the drums, Ricky Quisol. Then she introduced me to telecaster marvel and tenor J.B. Allison, David Phillips on pedal steel, and Jerry Logan on upright bass. At last she said, "And you've met Brian, right?" We looked at each other and smiled, then he turned to tune his guitar. Brian resembled a young Townes Van Zandt with his Western shirt and Levi's, shoulder-length hair, and soulful brown eyes. I sat down on a defunct speaker cabinet as the band warmed up. When I heard Brian sing, my toes curled inside my boots. He sounded like John Doe but with a generous dollop of Ray Price. My first sober crush turned my insides to jelly. His deep and sulky voice wrapped around me like a pelt, the scruff all warm and thick, and I wanted to sing with him real bad. He drove nails from a window up above all the while closing up the honky-tonks before returning to the green, green grass of home.

After the band ran through a handful of songs, they asked Tonette and me to sing what we had rehearsed. "Crazy Arms" was a good dance shuffle and "Apartment #9" was a sad, slow, tear-in-your-beer kind of song. We did a good enough job to be asked to sing with them during one of the three sets they'd be playing at their next regular Saturday-night gig at the DeMarco's 23 Club, a honky-tonk bar in Brisbane. I had not been this excited in a long time.

After rehearsal, J.B. Allison asked me to join him for dinner so we could talk about old times in Nashville. He had lived there in the 1970s, selling songs to Faron Young and Hank Williams Jr., winning songwriting contests, and even playing guitar in Jean Shepard's band. Trouble was his bag and I liked him plenty, but not as much as I liked Brian. I rode shotgun in J.B.'s truck and, as we drove away from Lennon Studios, we passed Brian loading out. He swung his guitar case over the side of his Ford pickup and set it in the bed, against the cab, then slid in behind the wheel. That's when I knew that dinner with J.B. meant just that, only dinner.

For the next week, all of my free time poured into getting ready for that Rounders gig in Brisbane. I thrifted with purpose. Since my booze weight and puffiness had vanished, I wanted to show off my tiny waistline in a cool vintage dress with cowboy boots, maybe even find a hat for the win. I found a see-through, dotted-swiss, baby-blue swing dress with pearl buttons on the bodice, and a chartreuse Hawaiian-print number that hugged my curves with three-quarter sleeves and a long zipper down the back. I fantasized about it being unzipped.

    I took myself to the movies to kill time before the gig. Standing on the sidewalk after a matinee showing of *Slingblade* at the Clay Theatre on Fillmore Street, I stood stock still on the sidewalk. All was quiet and peaceful for one blessed moment. Then a bird chattered and broke the spell. I laughed for no good reason, breathless and giddy, full of gratitude for how lucky I was to be sober and to see my silhouette on the brick wall of Wells Fargo as a playful shadow instead of a hopeless drunk.

    The night of the gig arrived and I experienced DeMarco's for the first time. It was a stroll through California country music history. The small town of Brisbane itself seemed stuck in Mayberry RFD time, and the club was an old roadhouse filled with assorted honky-tonk and rodeo memorabilia—all over the walls and behind its big wooden bar. Open since the 1940s, each decade since was represented in the mishmash decor: wagon wheels leaned up against the low-gated wrought-iron fence that corralled the stage; shitty 1970s trailer paneling held up neon beer and sports signs on the wall behind the stage; drop-down fluorescent lights lit the stage from above. The walls were dotted with signed photographs of dead celebrities, a stuffed bison head, bull horns, a plastic horse head, a velvet Elvis painting from his Hawaiian phase. Well worn, well used, well loved, and not meant to be kitschy.

    Before The Rounders started their sets, a local man in permanent-press Levi's and a black Stetson hat held a microphone and led a group of local senior citizens, mostly white and Filipino ladies, in line-dancing lessons. Once The Rounders set was under way, the dance floor swirled with old couples and tattooed rockabillies alongside drunk dirty dancers slumped over each other's shoulders, grinding hips during the ballads. They played plenty of Bakersfield shuffles and kept the boots swishing. When Tonette and I got up to sing with them, it felt effortless and surreal. I rode the current of their musicianship, weightless and exhilarated. After singing, I hunkered down in a booth and stared at Brian. I sang along with the harmonies on the choruses and when asked to dance, said no unless the person asking was Leonard Iniquez, the best dancer at DeMarco's. That man was light on his feet and could twirl anyone, even me, though I had no idea how to two-step. I'd found a version of honky-tonk heaven, sober and in California.

My life as an artist bloomed. I plugged away at the bass and wrote songs. Tonette made mixtapes for me to study all things country circa 1950 to 1970. We practiced a cappella in one or the other of our living rooms, and the high ceilings and wood floors produced a satisfying reverb. I idolized Graham Parsons and Emmylou Harris, and the current alt-country standouts like Lucinda Williams, Dwight Yoakam, Charlie (of course), and Steve Earle. It seemed like a lot of classic country music was more concerned with style than the substance I thought singer-songwriters expressed. Even so, I learned and got into classic country bass lines and harmonies from Tonette's mixtapes. The Blue Dolls were not an original band. We played covers. The retro-rockabilly scenesters were purists. That squeezed the life out of the way I wrote songs and even the way I dressed, but it drew a bigger crowd and turned out to be so much fun that I plunged into Wanda Jackson, the Davis Sisters, and Peggy Lee. Yet I yearned for a band where I could express myself more freely, maybe even a band centered around my songwriting.

We looked for a guitarist. We tried several people, but no one fit until we found John Stern, a rockabilly guitarist from Washington, DC, new to the thriving scene in San Francisco. The three of us became tight. When we weren't rehearsing, we hit the clubs and shows. We saw Merle Haggard at the War Memorial Building with Bonnie Owens singing backup. We saw Wanda Jackson on her secular tour, and we watched Dieselhed's rhythm section keep playing long after Link Wray fell off the stage at Bimbo's and broke his leg.

Keith called. He'd be touring through San Francisco soon. I told him the good news about getting sober and said of course I'd love to see him. Although he supported sobriety and applauded my learning the bass, he also felt compelled to warn me that the musician's life was full of disappointment, very little money, and long, boring hours. I didn't believe him. Kind of like I didn't believe Emmylou when she wondered why I wanted to move to Nashville to play country music, and how I had ignored Charlie when he reminded me about low audience turnouts on the road. These jaded fuckers weren't going to spoil my dream.

Swollen Appetite

Keith gave me a CD of Loretta Lynn and Conway Twitty greatest-duet hits because they had been his favorite as a kid. It was sweet to have sober sex with someone I knew and trusted. I adored his music and still cared about him. He was a good friend, and my friends were everything to me. I rode along with Keith to McCabe's in Santa Monica for a solo show. He shared the bill with none other than Charlie. That sonofabitch tried to kiss me even though that same ol' fiancée he still hadn't married waited in the wings. Matthew Sweet came to the show because Keith covered one of his songs, and I watched them argue about stupid shit in the green room. Now that I was sober and doing my own thing musically, I'd lost interest. I floated above the fray, more intrigued by my own music scene.

The Blue Dolls played our first full set at Edinburgh Castle a few days later. Against his manager's wishes, Keith played a short, word-of-mouth set before us and because of that, a good-sized crowd showed up. I wore my roommate Vassa's long, straight, red-haired wig with a red and white Partridge Family minidress. The PA was hinky, which worked for me because my throat was tight, clenched in fear from being both sober and on stage for the first time in front of Keith. Almost ready to play bass in public but not quite, we had a kooky and fun set with a pickup drummer and bass player. But this band was no Rounders.

Strange thing: once I pulled away from the unavailable men in my life, they tried to get closer. I became less and less interested in Keith and thought more and more about seeing Brian Mello in less than a week at the next Rounders gig in Brisbane.

Dear San Francisco music scene,

Let's dance. Put on your red shoes and dance the jump blues with me.

My sober life hummed. A slew of original songs poured out of me. I took long walks up and down Fillmore to recovery meetings in the Marina, and bass lines emerged: walking bass lines, country a-go-go, shuffles, 4/4s, waltzes. Melodies and lyrics followed. I wrote ideas down on anything I could find: blank edges of newsprint, napkins with blotted lipstick, greasy takeout paper bags, a notepad when I remembered to carry one. I made calls from phone booths to my message machine and sang melodic ideas lest I forget. I no longer felt estranged.

I discovered a new psychic on the corner of Hayes and Webster. I spoke a lot about Brian Mello and hoped the long, elegant fingers he used to strum the guitar strings would soon be used on me. The psychic said Brian had a secret, and the mystery put me in a tizzy. At the time my fantasy life favored hermaphrodites. Maybe that was Brian's secret?

The Rounders gigged often and invited the Blue Dolls to join them on stage on a regular basis, so I saw Brian more and more. I told Tonette to tell Ricky to tell Brian that I liked him. They never did. I wanted to make a move, but both my sponsor and my psychic told me to wait: be patient; do romance differently this time; quit being the seducer and be seduced for a change. I agonized but followed their advice. Turned out, Brian had not yet officially broken up with his last girlfriend, even though she had moved to Portland. That technicality drove me insane. The untapped passion went into my music.

Chapter 22 - You Can't Buy Experience

Throughout my time in San Francisco, I latched onto friends willing to help me record my demos. I appreciated their help, but the end results were unsatisfying. Brian Mello shared a studio space in San Jose with several other bands, including Texas Border Radio and The Bindlestiffs. A wizard of the four-track, he said he could help me record the new songs I was writing.

In the shared studio, with Brian's guitar slung low and his shy eyes averted, I plugged my bass into the amp. Genuinely decent, not the tiniest bit arrogant and yet so talented, Brian baffled me. In advance, I had sent cassettes of my songs with just the vocal and bass for him to learn before we recorded. I called my bass style, rudimentary at its best, the "tuba bass." Brian had learned my songs, and on track one he played the drums while I played bass. With just four tracks to work with, he bounced tracks and conserved. We fleshed out the remaining tracks with vocals, guitar, melodica, claves, and harmonies. Unafraid of big finishes and unconventional effects on simple country songs, Brian thoroughly satisfied my four-track needs. My all-over-the-place songwriting style suited him.

I headed south to record with Brian every few weeks, and over the course of a few months our relationship deepened. I began to edit my lyrical content in a way that let him know how ready I was, how available I was, and yet how understanding I could be of another's breakup process. I had never had a crush on a younger man before, so I teased him without mercy about having been a freshman when I was a senior in high school. Our goodbye hugs lasted a little too long, and we began to send mixtapes and poetry to each other via the mail. I looked in the brass box in my apartment vestibule after every work shift and checked my voicemail every ten minutes. Just in case. My every-so-often weekend Caltrain trips to San Jose reminded me of when I first moved to town and visited Greg before he died. Those train rides, all of them ending with Brian waiting for me, leaning against his Ford pickup outside the station, were provocative. My desire smoldered.

Brian drove to San Francisco midweek to see John Doe with me at the Bottom of the Hill. Just saying the title of John Doe's new CD, *Kissing So Hard*, felt erotic. I bought a black vintage 1940s silk slip with a tiny, moth-eaten hole an inch above my nipple, just beneath the hand-stitched edge. Fishnets and cowboy boots completed the ensemble—no jacket necessary on this rare warm night in The City. As we walked down the steps of my apartment building to Fell Street, Brian's hand grazed the small of my back.

He ordered me a Diet Coke and got a shot of tequila for himself but didn't finish it. Perplexed, I wondered about that half-swallow on the bar and the kind of person who could leave a drink unfinished. We moved as close to the stage as we could get. An arm's length away, John Doe hovered above us, sweaty, intense, and on. We writhed under his sweat. The lead singer from the Sunshine Club, Denise Bon Giovanni, and her hotter-than-shit girlfriend made out in front of us the whole time. I suffered like Anima Sola, the outcast soul in the flames of purgatory waving broken chains, as I swayed giddily in front of the stage and wished to be making out with Brian. He guided me by my slick shoulder when he walked me home afterward.

A month later, Keith returned to San Francisco and opened for Whiskeytown at the Great American Music Hall on O'Farrell, next to the infamous Mitchell Brothers strip club and a block away from the Phoenix Hotel. I had lost my dignity plenty of times drunk off my ass in that seedy little Bermuda Triangle of the Tenderloin. The other guitarist from The Rounders, J.B., had expressed interest in seeing Keith, and said he was more curious about my taste in men than in the music. I laughed and we went to the show together. Still haunted by that part of town, I was glad to have his company. J.B. diplomatically acknowledged the good musicianship. During Whiskeytown's set, one of us called them Whiskeydick because the lead singer tried too hard and annoyed us. "You can't buy experience," J.B. observed, and we laughed and laughed.

J.B. wished us a good night as I left the club with Keith. My desire was to channel some of the sexual deprivation I felt for Brian, since this retread action had worked for me and Keith the month before. But not this time. We got back to the Phoenix, and I just couldn't. I just couldn't keep having this kind of relationship. We parted as friends; Keith had always been a good friend. I felt rueful but sane on my cab ride home.

My romantic ties had to be severed if I wanted unfettered, new love. That's what my sponsor said, and that's what my heart told me. The very next time I saw Brian at a Rounders show at DeMarco's, I told him I'd broken off my relationship with Keith. He said his relationship with the woman in Portland had ended as well. Then I told him about an upcoming family visit to Florida and that I'd be gone for two weeks. Outside the club that night, Brian said he'd miss me. Then he bent down, brushed my hair to the side of my face with one of his long fingers, and kissed me. On the lips.

The first sober trip to see my family in Florida was not as difficult as past trips had been. My mom's bedroom in Orlando had two twin beds, and I bunked a nightstand away from her. Her snoring was astonishing. It kept me up, the worry and the noise, but I said the serenity prayer over and over and we didn't fight about it. I did not mention her weight or her drinking, although I did suggest she read some of my recovery literature, which she politely declined. I did not push. Florida seemed so wild and exotic now that I lived on the West Coast. On a beach trip with my brother, we saw a hammerhead shark dead on the jetty in Sebastian Inlet, and I dropped my camera in the warm waters trying to take a picture of my brother floating on his back. Later that afternoon on the white sands of Cocoa Beach in front of my grandmother's tiny pink cinderblock house, my teenage niece chased me with a pale yellow sand crab. To anyone who would listen, I swooned about recovery, more than a bit of an acolyte. Even so, it was a successful family visit where no one got hurt, and on the flight home I did not have a panic attack. I couldn't wait to get back to my scrumptious life in San Francisco. On that trip, I sent Vassa a postcard from Florida signed *Sandra Mello*.

Chapter 23 - First Date

Brian made an inspired choice for our first date: Buck Owens's Crystal Palace in Bakersfield. He picked me up in his teal four-cylinder Ford Ranger and we headed south down I-5 for 285 miles. We checked into the La Quinta next door, put on some fancier duds, and got to the restaurant in time to order fried chicken and biscuits before Buck hit the stage. I knew Buck Owens from *Hee-Haw*, a TV show my grandmother who lived in Cocoa Beach never missed. Brian had grown up in California's Central Valley listening to KUZZ, Buck's radio station.

    Several years earlier, in 1993, Buck had lost part of his tongue to throat cancer, so when he spoke, he lisped. But when he sang, his tenor had wings. While we ate dinner, Buck called one of the waitresses up on stage, and she sang Bonnie Tyler's hit "It's a Heartache," backed by the late-1990s version of the Buckaroos. She sounded exactly like Bonnie Tyler—a harried smoker with a smudged-lipstick game. She nailed what I love about country music: its practical poetry. I understood her world-weariness and day-old mascara.

The next morning, Brian asked if I wanted to meet his family, since they lived off Highway 99 in Visalia, right on our way back to the Bay Area. It was a mighty bold move. I said yes, all smug 'n' shit. I was going to meet the people who would become my new family on our very first date. The Mellos were sweet and fun-loving Portuguese Catholic walnut growers. They welcomed me with open arms and made it easy to love them right away.

We spent lots of time in the condo Brian shared with his roommate in San Jose, and the back of my head would fall asleep on his lumpy futon as we listened to *OK Computer* by Radiohead, Elliott Smith, Beck, Mark Eitzel, Morphine, Neko Case, Garbage, and the other Marilyn—Marilyn Manson. We rented the films *Amadeus*, *Clueless*, and *The Last Temptation of Christ* while eating dinner made with food from Trader Joe's. Brian, Nellie the cat, and I became a family. The three of us smooshed into my twin bed at the Fell Street apartment. Brian loved cats and got along well with Vassa and her many other pets in our flat. It's never easy to park in San Francisco, and sometimes, as we wound around the Fell Street neighborhood looking for spots, we shared a pint of Ben & Jerry's cookie dough ice cream. Ice cream had replaced my nightly whiskey, and we'd eat the whole pint before it melted. If, after an hour or so, we still couldn't find parking, Brian would park on the sidewalk under my bedroom window and pay the ticket if he got one. Some nights, in frustration, we turned the truck around and drove to the condo in San Jose instead.

Everyone knew Brian at the San Jose clubs, in particular at Fuel, located near the Greyhound station, and the Oasis. His former bands—The Jackdaws, Lonesome Weasels, and Susanna & The Goldenwest Playboys—had been fixtures of the rockabilly scene. Meeting Brian's friends and family plunked me into a whole new world, the life of my boyfriend. I had not been invited into such intimate realms since my marriage with Brad. The Loretta Lynn song "Walk through This World with Me" became our soundtrack.

Dumbfounded by the gifts of sobriety, especially an exciting romantic relationship, I was more than willing to work hard to stay sober. I had too much good shit to lose. But being sober meant telling the truth about all kinds of stuff one might prefer to not talk about.

Sex is one of the best things about having a body, and I loved it. But it had not always been great with other people. Prone to exaggerate in past sexual relations, I was determined to be honest with Brian. It was more important to me to not swindle myself. The reasons why I faked orgasms in the past could fill a page: I wasn't excited enough to climax; I was ready to be done with it and sleep; my partner was selfish; my partner was unskilled; I did not want my partner to feel bad when I didn't come. (I could make them feel bad later.) Plenty of times I was too stressed, too drunk, too anxious, too uninterested, too unable to communicate my needs, too embarrassed by how long it took me, or too impatient with myself and partners to wait for it. Faking orgasms moved things along, and I could take care of myself later.

It didn't take any time at all for Brian and me to get the hang of things. The impulse to fake anything slipped away.

Dear Alcohol,
I would have missed all of this.
I was going to let you kill me.

The sober life kept surprising me with its mercy. For seventeen years an apple had sat on the top of my head, and I had faced the archer with my eyes closed and a bottle to my lips. The appreciation for my job, my friends, my family, San Francisco, and my new bands, the Blue Dolls and The Rounders, swelled. My idea factory cranked nonstop. A song flowered petal by petal, note by note, in just minutes. The song wrote itself. It was so easy, I thought the song must have been something I'd learned earlier in life and had forgotten until now because it was too sweet and too corny to be mine. But when I sang it for others, they assured me it was new, that I had written it.

I saw it coming, then I saw it go

Digging for answers I already know

Eyes on the heavens, feet on the earth

Life is revealing all of its worth

Loving arms around me feel like my own

We're in this together, not alone

If there is true love, how will I find it?

Glowing like diamonds or coal in the mine

I was in love with Brian Mello. We spent every not-working minute together. We would load up the truck after a gig at DeMarco's and watch milky fingers of fog crawl over the midnight-blue peaks of hills that separated Highway 101 from the Pacific. Or we'd drive over redwood-studded hills through La Honda on our way to a daytime gig at the San Gregorio General Store. Once Brian pointed out Apple Jacks Inn, a sketchy-looking biker bar, and said The Jackdaws had gigged there. As he described that old band of his, I gasped and told him I had seen them at the Blue Lamp a few years back, as drunk as a skunk! How strange and exciting this life—that our paths had crossed again when things careened in just the right direction—a way that let you know someone mattered. Sympatico, synchronicity, good timing, and grace all seemed like the same thing to me, and I was in awe of all of it.

We took arty photos of each other. We wrote more poetry. My dream to become a successful artist had a slippery tail. But thank God I had a new version of that dream. We played a few duo shows as Austin Mello, where we sang the new, original songs we demoed. We opened for Victoria Williams, and for Chuck Prophet and Stephanie Finch. We saw Radiohead at the Warfield on the *OK Computer* tour. I wore Vassa's tall black leather boots and short white vinyl miniskirt. We parked on Mission Street just two blocks over from the Warfield, where I had worked during some of my first months in San Francisco, inebriated. Now stone-cold sober, the show flooded my senses. On fire with love and a new lease on life, I felt ten feet tall.

Victor called and said he'd be in the Bay Area soon and asked if I wanted to join him at the Mystic Theatre in Petaluma. Emmylou was touring *Wrecking Ball* with her band, Spyboy. I couldn't not say yes. But I asked for two tickets: one for me and one for my boyfriend. I don't remember the conversation exactly, but Victor said okay, he'd put my name plus one at will call. When Brian and I got to Petaluma that night, we were not on the list. And Victor declined to attend that particular show. The staff at the Mystic let us in anyway, even though the show had sold out. We sat on the very top step of the middle aisle, against the rafters. Getting in without Victor's help made the show all the more glorious. It felt good to drop that thorny relationship.

Sober for a little over a year, I figured if I needed a spiritual path, so must my partner. My sponsor and I went to see Betty Bethard one more time at the Unitarian Church, and I got there early enough to ask her the question.

"Since it's important to my sobriety that I follow a spiritual path, should I encourage my new boyfriend to follow a spiritual path with me?"

Betty replied: "The spiritual path to encourage is your own. The man you worry about *sits at the right hand of God*."

Hell yeah, he did.

Chapter 24 – Oakland

We wanted to live together.

The first dot-com boom of the late 1990s had made San Francisco unaffordable. We needed to find a place in between our two jobs. I worked in Japantown at the Miyako, and Brian worked as a graphic artist in Livermore. As much as I did not want to leave the city I dearly loved, and where my sober roots were deepening, Oakland seemed like a practical location and one we could better afford. I needed to be walking distance to a BART station since I did not have a car, so I researched ads for rentals near Rockridge.

With a red felt-tip pen, I circled newspaper ads for one-bedroom apartments. I sat in the classic diner atmosphere of the Rockridge Cafe and ate chocolate soufflé pie and sipped French roast while I waited for apartment managers to show what was available. There were lines around the block at every open house. These apartments were nothing special—not like San Francisco's gorgeous, albeit dilapidated, Victorian and Edwardian buildings. I met with the manager of one of the typical, sagging complexes built in the late 1950s and early 1960s that covered Oakland's hillsides. He told me they had two apartments available: one right by the front door on the street, and one on the backside of the building, tucked into a corner of the rambling garden with its kidney-shaped pool. Brian and I took the one in the back; it was under two mighty palm trees and an overgrown jade plant hedge that sheltered salamanders under its thick stems. A bullet hole had splintered into an asterisk in the sliding glass patio door a foot above the beige carpet; rumor had it a jealous fight had taken place between two Raiders cheerleaders over the same football player, and a gunfight ensued. Yet the apartment charmed us with its 1960s accents, like a teakwood wall divider between the kitchen and the front door, brass V-shaped cabinet pulls, and a built-in bookshelf in the living room. Big and boxy, it had a huge front closet where we could store our music gear and coats, as well as plenty of linen cabinet space in the bathroom. For $850 a month, it could work as a stepping stone to a better place down the line.

  On the day after Thanksgiving 1997, at my apartment on Fell Street, a month before we moved into the Oakland apartment, Brian parked his Ford Ranger on the sidewalk below my bedroom window. By the side of my twin bed, he knelt on one knee and asked me to marry him. I said yes to another new beginning where my dearheart had not known me drunk.

  I began to prepare for the move. In my last bedroom in San Francisco, I knelt down to pull my suitcase out from under the bed, then cradled my head in my arms over the bedspread and prayed.

Thank you Alcoholism,
You got me to San Francisco.

Thank you Higher Power,
You got me sober and I can call myself an artist without snickering.

A few months later, I called the Inyo County courthouse from the bedroom floor of our new Oakland apartment, legs splayed in a V, taunting Nellie with a peacock feather. An appointment was made for us to be married by a judge in Death Valley on my thirty-fifth birthday. A few minutes later, the phone rang and the judge apologized for not realizing that date was Easter Sunday, and she'd be out of town. Bummed, Brian and I adjusted our plan. We'd still spend the night at the Stovepipe Wells Village Hotel in Death Valley and see Zabriskie Point, but we would do so on the drive into Las Vegas, where we'd get married at the first chapel I called that had an open reservation: the Little Church of the West.

In our new neighborhood, I shopped for a vintage wedding dress. At Madame Butterfly's Vintage Clothing Store on College Avenue I found a gorgeous 1940s eggshell-colored floor-length princess-waist number. But I noticed that the fabric in the sleeves was frayed and tight, about to rip. I scored a different used 1940s-style long satin dress cut on the bias just down the street at the newly opened Crossroads Trading Company. Brian found his outfit at a Western wear store on Telegraph that was going out of business: a priced-to-move Trego's Westwear three-piece permanent-press suit in dark brown with baby-blue pinstripes.

On Friday, April 10, 1998, we drove south to Bakersfield in the Ford Ranger, now fondly dubbed the Teal Chariot, with an overnight bag stashed behind the bench seat and our wedding duds hanging from the window hooks. At the Crystal Palace, before Buck Owens's early show, we ordered fried chicken dinners, just like we had on our first date, and sent a request written on a napkin to Buck via our waitress. Fond of taking requests, Buck read our note, strummed his guitar, and sang the chorus to Tammy Wynette's hit single, "D-I-V-O-R-C-E." Then he threw his head back in his infamous *Hee-Haw* laugh—just kidding!—and wished us well before the Buckaroos launched into our song, "Storms Never Last."

Back on the road by seven, we drove through an industrial area of Bakersfield, past refineries on the dusty outskirts of town where the sand had drifted onto the roadside and the landscape consisted of the occasional shaggy palm tree or nothing at all. We had 218 miles to go on CA 58 before our next turn. Far away from any city lights on a two-lane highway illuminated by the moon and our headlights, we listened to music and talked, and smoked the occasional American Spirit cigarette. It was eerie, the endless dark and winding road climbing a subtle grade. A single light beckoned three hours later, a closed gas station and tiny road sign indicating the turnoff to our hotel. Those ten miles of serpentine road narrowed and descended steeply. Brian geared down and I gripped the armrest so hard my arm was sore the next day.

Swollen Appetite

A giant sign—No Potable Water—caught our attention as we pulled into the hotel parking lot, which had materialized all at once in the moonlight. Strange people in shorts meandered drunkenly across the dark road in front of us as they wandered from the dimly lit saloon/store/outpost across the street. We overheard German being spoken as we got out and stretched, then took our bag and wedding garments to the lobby to check in. Things got even weirder inside the rental office. Behind the counter stood a tall skinny man and a short round woman with very few teeth. "We weren't sure if you were gonna make it," the tall man said, as the woman gave us an uninhibited smile. We signed the register. They handed us our key and we walked, spooked out and tired, to our room.

We opened the door and found two people having sex in our bed. We shut the door fast, headed back to the office, and asked for an unoccupied room. The woman laughed. "Oh, the bar must be closing. Couples sneak into the empty rooms." She handed us different keys—to a room where we found an older couple asleep. The light from the hallway woke the woman and she scrambled up, afraid: "Oh no!"

Jittery, upset, and tired, we apologized and asked for yet another room, but the hotel was all booked up. Although: "There is one tiny room that we use as a storage closet," the tall man offered. We were too exhausted to refuse. The curtainless storage closet had a twin bed and was lit by the full moon. It was too dirty to take our socks off.

After an unexpected and delicious breakfast in the semi-swanky hotel restaurant we drove to Vegas, stopping often to take pictures of the remarkable landscape: Devil's Haystacks, Zabriskie Point, Death Valley Junction. Under the hot morning sun, we crossed the state line into Pahrump, Nevada, and a rock flew up and cracked our windshield. We didn't care. It wasn't a white owl warning us in white owl country. We were on our way to Vegas to get hitched! Jacked on coffee and love, we got cleaned up in the hotel room at Binion's Horseshoe Casino, then headed to the courthouse for a marriage license. The line moved quickly. The two couples ahead of us were dressed in thrift-store wedding garb. We drove to the Little Church of the West, the very chapel where Elvis married Ann-Margret in *Viva Las Vegas*. The minister delivered a moving ceremony. I cried and Brian wiped the tears from my cheek before we kissed and became husband and wife. The photographer positioned us in high school prom poses and asked if we were part of the Rockabilly Roundup happening downtown.

    We went back to Binion's and hung up our wedding garb, took our sweet time consummating our nuptials, put on Levi's, and roamed around the casinos. We played the slots, ate buffet, then consummated our nuptials again before falling asleep, happy and exhausted in our giant wedding bed with a view of the Strip.

But—before all that happened—we'd moved the week before Christmas 1997 into our Oakland apartment. We loaded up the Teal Chariot with my worldly possessions. We said goodbye to my darling roommate, Vassa, and the various critters. I was glad I'd keep a toehold in San

Francisco with my job at the Miyako. We bungee-corded my Ficus, fertilized and stronger from all the times I peed in it when I didn't want to stop raging on the phone, up against the truck's cab. My bass and amp and boxes of books, demos, CDs, and clothes buttressed the tall plant. Nellie spoke in tongues in her cat carrier, and both of us tried to soothe her. Not running away from anything this time, we sailed over the Bay Bridge. Ficus leaves flew from the branches of my tree. From the side mirror I watched, unworried. I knew they would grow back.

Dear San Francisco,
I see you from across the Bay at the ATM near our apartment.

The inspiration for Swollen Appetite

Since 1996, I have been telling a 15-minute version of this memoir in a setting with others like me who seek support for alcohol use disorder. We tend to have attention and anxiety issues as well, and once upon a time, in the 1940s, when this support group came into existence, those 15 minutes were called a pitch. Uniquely qualified, we break down our personal stories into bite-sized pieces: what it was like when we were using, what happened, and what it's like now that we're sober.

I needed more time. I needed to pull the corners of my page across a parking lot and cover it with story after story. To not have to convince anyone of anything other than reading the next page. The brave woman I was in the 1990s needed more attention than I could give her. She took a lot of chances and risked her life to get me to where I am now: alive and creative. Swollen Appetite is my amends to her - a woman out of her depth and mind - but damn, wasn't she something?

Disclaimers

I changed the names of some folks but not others. For those with whom I had serious relationships or anyone I thought might want their identity protected, I gave a pseudonym. It's tricky talking about the past. There's no factual way to describe a perspective or a memory. I rendered from old journals written by a drunk and emotionally distraught narrator, my first 4th Step, a mountain of out-of-focus photographs, and a few precious letters. There are actual recordings of poems I wrote in the '90s from old cassette tapes that I transferred to digital and loaded onto my website, even though they make me cringe. I owed the reader/listener the real deal. There are no videos, no transcripts, no documented proof that I felt like what I said I felt like. Or that you said what I said you said. There's just me telling the reader what I know about myself way back when. I hope it makes you think about yourself when you were on the cusp of becoming whoever you became.

Many people who were a part of my life, sometimes a big part of my life, did not make it into this book. It wasn't because I didn't remember them, or they weren't important. I chose whom to include based on keeping the story moving. Several folks don't look too good in this telling, especially me. Whatever category you fall into, know that I love you or, at the very least, want to thank you for being in my life. The light that flared when you set your souls on fire lit my way home.

Thank you –

San Francisco for dazzling me.

The readers: Beth Lisick, Jack Boulware, Chuck Prophet, Francie and John Raeside, Laura Cavaluzzo and Pete Craft, Wendy Newman, Rebecca Coseboom, Shermann Min, as well as a bevy of awesome broads who took in the first 50 pages back in the wee days of COVID: Sally Mudd, Wendy Brazill, Jill Olson, Beth McKenna, Julie Kramer, Cori

Crooks, and Deborah Crooks. Your encouragement and pointers kept me honest.

Melanie Berdofe and Jim Kelly, your generosity, friendship, and the decency you shared by paying your employees to not work in the early months of the COVID-19 lockdown provided me not only with groceries and rent but also a blessed writing retreat!

Lindsey Westbrook, my beloved copy editor. I'm sorry that I continually changed the manuscript post edit. Thank you for your time, patience, and talent. I'd be sunk without you.

Marissa Hereso, for all the walks and talks that gladdened my heart. Thanks for sharing your Figma Moodboard with me!

Laura Cavaluzzo, for all the impromptu copy edits of blurbs and such. You make writing look easy.

Jessica Gruner, for your eagerness to read and willingness to proof.

Sally and Mina Mudd and Gary McCormick for the quiet room to record Chapters 3 and 5.

Margaret Belton and Dave Cuetter, for the pro tips for recording and polishing the audio tracks.

Laura Clemons, for being my writer-sister and my sister-sister. I need you as a sounding board.

Kathryn Kruse, for editing the first draft. You noticed the lack of shame that '90s Sandra demonstrated in those early pages, and since the goal was to stay in that time, without the meddling of hindsight, wouldn't she have felt more shame for her behavior? (What a testament to recovery that I forgot shame in the early drafts!) I will always be grateful for our work together on WHAT YOU CARRY.

Adena Gilbert, you're a friggin' saint for listening to the fears that plagued me while writing. Your humor, tenderness, and guidance have kept me sane and able to look not only myself but others in the eyes.

Brian Mello, everything's better because of you - the cover art, help with the audiobook, and the clever marketing pieces. You're good company. Hearing you rehearse music in the other room fills my heart and reminds me how lucky I am to get to walk through this world with you.

Unsolicited advice:

If you think you have a problem with substance abuse, you are not alone. Get help; you'll be amazed before you're halfway through.

About the Author

As a songwriter, Mello has created, recorded, performed, toured and published original music, in the band, The Bellyachers. It has been featured in television and film. She published her first novel, WHAT YOU CARRY in 2018 and lives in the Bay Area of CA with her musician husband and obstinate cat.

www.ingramcontent.com/pod-product-compliance
Lightning Source LLC
Chambersburg PA
CBHW010447010526
44118CB00021B/2528